Writing
and
Being

Writing
and
Being

*Embracing Your Life
through Creative Journaling*

G. Lynn Nelson

New World Library
Novato, California

New World Library
14 Pamaron Way
Novato, California 94949
www.newworldlibrary.com

Cover design by Paul Goldstein
Book design by Suzanne Albertson

Publisher Cataloging-in-Publication Data
Nelson, G. Lynn.
Writing and being : embracing your life through creative journaling /
G. Lynn Nelson. — Rev. ed.
p.   cm.
Includes bibliographical references and index.
ISBN 978-1-880913-61-1 (pbk.)
1. English language—Rhetoric—Psychological aspects.
2. Diaries—Authorship—Problems, exercises, etc. I. Title.

PE1408 .N46 2004
808/.042/019—dc22   0409

Printed on recycled paper

Grateful acknowledgment is made for permission to reprint the following copyrighted material:
Excerpt from *Anne Frank: The Diary of a Young Girl* by Anne Frank. ©1952 by Otto H. Frank. Reprinted by permission of Doubleday, a division of Bantam Doubleday Dell Publishing Group, Inc.

Excerpt from *The Three-Pound Universe* by Judith Hooper and Dick Teresi. ©1986 by Judith Hooper and Dick Teresi. Reprinted with the permission of Macmillan Publishing Company.

Excerpt from *Raids on the Unspeakable* by Thomas Merton. ©1964 by The Abbey of Gethsemani, Inc. Reprinted by permission of New Directions.

Excerpt from *House Made of Dawn* by N. Scott Momaday. ©1966, 1967, 1968 by N. Scott Momaday. Reprinted by permission of HarperCollins Publishers, Inc.

Excerpt from *Zen Mind, Beginner's Mind* by Shunryu Suzuki. Reprinted by permission of Weatherhill Publishing, Inc.

Excerpt from *Directions for the Contemplative Life* by Meister Eckhart.

To my mother and father, Leah and Herb,
who grounded my life in love;

and to Lorrie, Amanda, and Robin,
whose love sustains me now.

Contents

Invocation

Humankind has not woven the web of life. We are but one thread within it. Whatever we do to the web we do to ourselves. All things are bound together. All things connect. Whatever befalls the earth befalls the children of the earth.
—CHIEF SEATTLE, 1855

Sunday morning, I drove out to the reservation, to Simon's place. I parked my truck beside his old adobe house that blends with the desert, turned off the engine, and sat for awhile in the sunshine and silence. The engine ticked; a fly buzzed; a lizard scurried beneath a creosote bush. The dog came first—tail wagging, smiling. I scratched his ears and talked to him. Then Simon appeared, walking in from the trail that leads back to his ceremonial grounds in the desert. His long, raven hair was pulled back in a ponytail. As always, his dark Apache face was open and clear and friendly. We shook hands, gently.

He rode along to show me where to find some willows for the meditation hogan I was building in my backyard, in Tempe. As we drove down a back trail past some desert land that was being bulldozed for irrigation and crops, Simon pointed to a lone cottonwood tree in the distance. "There's a hawk nest in that tree," he said quietly. "They raised two babies this spring. I was afraid the farms people would bulldoze it."

As we got closer, I could see the nest high in the tree—and a large red-tailed hawk on a branch nearby. About twenty yards out from the tree in each of the four directions, someone had placed tall branch-poles in the ground. From the top of each branch fluttered a small rag of color marking one of the sacred directions. And the bulldozers had turned aside.

The culture I was born into—the dominant, left-brained, technological culture—is too often a bulldozer. And when I am not careful (full of care), it makes of me a bulldozer without my even knowing. But when I am quiet and attentive, I see the colored rags flying everywhere, saying, "This, too, is sacred."

May our time here together
be quiet and attentive;
may it lead us toward seeing the sacred,
toward hearing the silence,
toward meeting the light
which is coming over the hills.

All my relations . . . .
—GLN

Introduction

*In the white man's world, language . . . has undergone a
process of change. . . . His regard for language—for the Word
itself—as an instrument of creation has diminished nearly to
the point of no return. It may be that he will perish by the
word.*

—N. SCOTT MOMADAY,
HOUSE MADE OF DAWN

Taking Back the Gift of Language

This is not a book about writing. This is a book about people writing. It is about writing as a tool for intellectual, psychological, and spiritual growth. It is about our language and our being and their powerful interconnectedness, which have often been taken away from us without our even knowing what we have lost. This book is about taking back the miraculous gift of our language and using it as an instrument of creation.

Ultimately, this book is about finding peace and love in our hearts. That sounds idealistic and grandiose, I know. Still, I have to say it—because I see it happen all the time in the lives of my students and I feel its movement in my heart. My colleagues down the halls of the English department would snort and roll their eyes at words like "peace" and "love" in connection with writing—just as they already look askance at a course called "Writing and Being." But I have been teaching such a course for almost ten years, and each semester I voluntarily teach an extra section of it—and still I have to turn students away. For the most part, these students do not come for a grade or a degree. They come because, in a left-brained institution in a left-brained land, their hearts are starved. They come because they have heard about a course where you write for reasons beyond critical analysis and correctness, where you write to tell your own stories, to heal your wounds, to find a bit of peace and love.

Too often in school, we study language and writing in isolation, apart from the people who speak and write and apart from what happens when people speak and write—apart from our being. This is rather like studying the skeleton of a bird: The skeleton is, in limited ways, edifying and interesting, but it is dead. Such isolated language has no heart. Its true purposes and its real value are no longer there. It cannot fly nor sing.

To talk about writing apart from the people who do it, apart from their being, is to put writing in a small box and remove the wonder and the magic and the power from it. For the instructor, it is to play sad little games with language—circling misspelled words and dangling participles, making students feel small and stupid, and turning them away from the power of their own words.

My workshops, classes, and this book are about taking back the gift of our language as an instrument of creation. To do that, we must first remind ourselves that language is not a subject we study in school—that is just one small thing we have done with it. I long ago noticed an interesting phenomenon. When I meet people for the first time and they ask me what I do, if I tell the truth and say, "I am an English teacher," almost invariably they apologize, muttering something like, "Oh, I was never very good at that." Then they become obviously uncomfortable around me, assuming I am listening intently for their mistakes in grammar and pronunciation (as they believe is the job of any good English teacher) and sidle away from me to go off and talk to a real person.

And I want to grab them like the zealot I am and say, "Oh, no, it is not like that at all!" Language is a mystery and a miracle that has been given to us we know not why. Some time between 100,000 and 40,000 years ago, the cerebral cortex blossomed in the human cranial cavity like some exotic flower and along with it came language—this amazing ability to make sounds and marks that enable us to convey meaning to one another and with which we might explore the universe within and without.

By the time we reach four years old, we already have a level of language beyond the explaining and understanding and research of all the "experts" in education. And no one knows why, between the ages of one and four, language emerges from within each of us, why we become incredibly, amazingly proficient at language without ever cracking a grammar book or taking a test or even meeting an English teacher. But it happens. The gift of language emerges within us and waits there for us to find its power. That is what this book is about: taking back our lives through the power of language.

I have not always been aware of the power of language. For a long time, through my teaching and my writing, I have been finding my way to the power of writing and being. And I still have far to go. But my students keep teaching me and my journal keeps showing me the way.

A Lesson in Language

The first year I taught high school English, I set up nice straight rows of desks in my classroom, because I had been told that nice straight rows were what life and education were all about (and I used to believe what I was told). At the end of one of those rows, on certain days, there sat a rather nondescript and tattered-looking girl in my sophomore English class. I say "on certain days" because she was often absent. And even when she was there, she couldn't tell an adjective from a noun. What's more, she didn't care.

Her attitude incensed me. I had spent four years preparing to show her the difference between an adjective and a noun: She had no right not to care. Looking back, I see that my disgust with her, and others like her, went well beyond my opinion of her grammar; it bordered on a kind of elitist and moral condemnation of the total person. I did not know the total person, of course (straight rows prevent that kind of thing), but my feelings seemed justified by her apathy toward those things that I was prepared to make my life's work. With my red pen, I attacked her pitiful papers with righteous indignation.

But in about the middle of the semester, she didn't show up at all for two weeks. By Friday of the second week, I decided to check on her. In the school office, I was informed that the girl's mother had died and that she had gone to live with an uncle.

I was secretly relieved to hear that she was gone, for though I would not have admitted it then, she and others like her gave me a vague uneasiness about myself and my profession and my nice straight rows. For some reason, however—probably because of that same uneasiness—I copied down the girl's address from the files before I left the office.

One Sunday afternoon, my wife and I went for a drive, and I decided to go by the student's address. It was not easy to find. We finally found it on the edge of town, a dead house among a scattering of dilapidated and dying houses near the new freeway. It was deserted. An old man sat smoking his pipe on the porch of the house next door. I stopped the car and went to talk to him. Something more than mere curiosity was driving me by then.

The old man said that the woman who lived in that house had died about two weeks ago. She was a divorced woman, he informed me, and an alcoholic, living there with her three kids—the oldest daughter was in high school and took care of the younger two, if anybody did. In fact, he offered with a kind of grim enjoyment, since the mother worked swing shift and then went out every night and was usually in a drunken sleep in the morning when the kids got themselves off to school, it turned out that she had lain dead in her bedroom for two days before anyone discovered her. . .

I left abruptly.

The following Monday, not quite so abruptly (because I was not sure where I was going), my students and I began leaving adjectives and nouns and nice straight rows. For I knew then that if I were going to continue to teach, I had to offer my students more than the meager little box of language I had been trained to give. I knew that both they and I desperately needed something we could take home with us, something that would help us survive and grow and find meaning in the whirling world outside our classroom. So that Monday, not knowing quite what we were doing, my students and I started writing in journals, writing from our hearts.

That was many years ago, and with each passing year, I have gotten farther from that narrow view of language that could not help the tattered girl. Since that time, I have taught high school, worked in some elementary schools, gone to graduate school, lived for four years with six mentally disabled children, moved to Arizona to teach at the university, started a school for dropout kids on the Gila River Reservation, become director of the Greater Phoenix Area Writing Project, and given hundreds of writing workshops. Nothing in those experiences, with the exception of a few comfortable colleagues and several uncomfortable administrators, has suggested that it would be better to go back to those straight rows and that little view of language. With every year, with every class, with every workshop, with every journal I fill with words, I have wandered deeper into the mystery and wonder and power of the word as an instrument of creation.

So, I tell you at the beginning of this book what I tell my students at the beginning of my writing classes: Here is what I hope you will get from this book. Ten years from now, I hope you will be sitting up some night at midnight under the light at the kitchen table—writing. Not because you have a paper due the next day or because someone has given you an assignment—but because you are hurting or grieving or confused, or because you are collecting some of the small joys of your day, or because you need to let go of some anger. Whatever the reason, you'll be sitting there at that table writing because you are a writer. My wish is for you to be a life-long writer. My hope is that writing will be a tool—an emotional, intellectual, and spiritual tool—to help you survive and grow and find meaning and purpose and peace in your life.

I see all of these things happening in the lives of people as they enter the river of their writing and being. As I write this introduction, I have just finished another semester of writing workshops and my "Writing and Being" and first-year composition classes for Native American students. Once again, my students' writings from the end of the class affirm my belief in the power of this process. Here are a few excerpts from their closing statements:

> I reread the letter I wrote to myself a million years ago back in September[1]. . . . Somehow, a big thorn has been extracted from my heart. I don't have all the answers, but I don't have as many questions either.
>
> My writing now allows me to laugh, sing, and cry.
>
> My spiritual awareness is growing and I'm beginning to feel abundance of some sort. . . . Writing is magic.
>
> When I reread my letter to myself, the biggest change I noticed was how much more peaceful I feel now. There was some strong anger in my life, and I felt scattered. Now I am feeling so much more focused. . . . I feel like I have befriended myself again.

Writing is a healing and creative journey back to the mystery and power of our words as an instrument of creation that came latent within us at birth. It is a path with a heart. The people who wrote the com-

---

1. I have my students write a letter to themselves at the beginning of the semester to be opened and read at the end of the semester.

ments above are on that journey, and this book will help you along that path, also.

A Brief Overview

Each of the ten chapters that follow discusses a dimension of the writing-and-being process. Each also contains guided "Explorations" for journal writing and suggestions for public writing.

Chapter 1, "Beginning Your Journey," talks about the logistics of journal keeping and contains some suggestions to get you started.

Chapter 2, "Entering the River," looks at the whole writing process and helps you see the relationship between personal and public writing.

Chapter 3, "Seeking Silence," explores the need for stillness between words, touching on the relationship between writing and meditation.

Chapter 4, "Letting Go," examines the value of being nonjudgmental in writing and being, of having "soft eyes" and a beginner's mind.

Chapter 5, "Centering in the Self," looks at what happens within when you write in your journal and how journal writing leads to spiritual growth.

Chapter 6, "Exploring the Kingdom Within," focuses on the amazing human brain and how new understandings about the brain confirm the power of journal writing.

Chapter 7, "Writing and Healing," explores the power of journal writing to help heal psychological and spiritual wounds.

Chapter 8, "Seeking Community," describes the basic elements of a true caring community and how being part of one can fill you with positive energy.

Chapter 9, "Taking Back Our Hearts," shares a story about my Native American students and their writing as an example of how the Feather Circle of writing ripples outward in love.

Chapter 10, "Closing," is simply my good-bye to you by telling a story.

The guided Explorations that follow each chapter embody the heart of this book's purpose. The Explorations lead you into doing the work that must be done to bring about changes in your writing and your being. Because they are open-ended and adaptable, and because you are always changing, you can do these Explorations over and over again, and they will continue to yield new ways of seeing and saying for you.

All the Explorations begin by asking you to go inside yourself, to start with your heart, to take your stories out from within and look at them and learn from them. Starting in Chapter 3, the Explorations also contain a dimension called "Toward Public Writing." This section suggests ways to give your journal work new form as meaningful writing to be shared with others. Thus, while this book is primarily about personal journal writing, since that work grounds you in the source of all meaningful writing, the ideas presented here can help you create powerful and effective public writing as well. Writing teachers and aspiring public writers will find here a most powerful tool.

You can readily find your way through this book and into the writing process alone. I wish for you, however, a writing-and-being support group or a soft-eyed, caring class to travel beside you on this journey. Such a community is not necessary, but it adds a powerful dimension.

In any case, my hope is that, whether you are new to journal writing or have been carrying your journal around for years, you will find herein encouragement, support, and inspiration for your writing and being.

one

Beginning Your Journey

I hope that I shall be able to confide in you completely, as I have never been able to do in anyone before, and I hope that you will be a great support and comfort to me.

—ANNE FRANK, INSCRIPTION AT THE
BEGINNING OF HER JOURNAL

A Private Place

Your journal is your private place, a room of your own. Your journal can be anything from loose sheets of paper in a folder to a grade-school tablet to a seventy-dollar, leather-bound, gold-embossed, parchment-paper book. The only real criterion for your personal journal—and you need to attend to it carefully—is that it is something you feel comfortable writing in, something that invites you in and does not intimidate you. For this and other reasons, I often suggest to beginning journal keepers, "Let a journal find you."

In the usual hard-eyed, left-brained approach, you would march to the bookstore, commandeer something that looks "appropriate" and "proper," and buy it—all without attending to the process or to your needs and feelings.

Letting a journal find you is quite a different matter. You begin by reminding yourself that you need a journal—but you do not box up or limit what you "should" get or what might be "proper" or where it might find you. Instead, you maintain soft eyes (openness and acceptance) and a beginner's mind; simply be aware that you need a journal. And then wait for one to find you.

You may have to help the process along a little, at least this early in the game, by exposing yourself to some journals—that is, by hanging around places where there are potential journals (bookstores, stationery stores, department stores). But even then you can let the process work by not forcing it, by attending to how each potential journal feels to you, by waiting for one to catch your eye or whisper to you. In this way, before you have even begun to write, you will be practicing new and larger ways of being and knowing and responding.

Your journal will be one that feels good to you, one that invites you to write in it. From my experience and needs, here are some thoughts about the physical aspects of my journal that you might want to consider:

- Since my journal goes with me everywhere, usually in my backpack, it must be hard-backed and durable.

- For me, a good journal is one that is well-bound but will still open relatively flat without a big roll in the pages toward the binding.

- I have grown to prefer unlined pages and paper of good quality (and preferably recycled). Check your own feelings about lined pages.

- I prefer a fairly large journal—at least approaching 8½-by-11-inch pages—for several reasons. I often tape into my journal things I have written or typed elsewhere. Similarly, I sometimes tape into my journal letters I have received, pictures, notes, quotations, etc. I like to draw, diagram, and doodle in my journal. I like to leave fairly large margins so I can label things I might want to locate later (e.g., dreams; ideas related to an article, story, or poem; an image or memory; references to particular people). Large margins also allow me to record further feelings and observations that occur to me when I read over my journal entries at a later date.

These are just a few of the things I have come to look for in a good, comfortable, functional journal. You will have your own needs. Attend to them.

No Critics

As you write in your journal, you will need to keep reminding yourself that this is not the time or the place to worry about things like spelling, punctuation, grammar, complete sentences, and so on. These rules and conventions have evolved to ensure some consistency in public writing, to aid in our communication with one another. But they should not be a concern in your journal. Attending to such things will only impede the process of your writing—the free and spontaneous flow of words from within you. The only rule for your journal writing is that whatever works for you is valid.

Even though it may be difficult at first, when you write in your journal, do not be concerned about neatness and "proper" mechanics and conventions. These are editorial concerns. They need to be applied rigorously only near the end of the writing process, after you have explored and evolved the content in your journal, and only when and if you want to turn it into public writing, that is, to share some of your words with someone else.

And you will want to share them. That is almost inevitable when you enter this process with your heart. For you will begin to see things and say things and know things and feel things that will amaze you. And you will feel your own voice emerging in your words—as unique and distinct as your fingerprints or your DNA pattern. You will want to share your words because you will have something to say, something worth sharing, something meaningful and helpful and careful—gifts from your heart.

But until that point, until something from your journal wants to work its way out and into public writing, there are no rules or standards that need concern you. Any serious attention to them earlier in the process will only distract you from much more important concerns. In your journal writing, whenever you find "critics" sitting on your shoulder and whispering in your ear ("messy penmanship" . . . "misspelled word" . . . "you forgot to put your name in the upper right-hand corner" . . . "incomplete sentence"), just give them a good whack and carry on.

Looking through my journals, I can find no entries that strike me as "typical" of the kind or style of writing I do there. Some pages contain a stream-of-consciousness flow of words with little punctuation. Many pages are hodgepodges of notes, observations, and feelings; jumbles of styles and penmanship; collages of words and drawings.

My journal is more like a storage room or a secret hideaway than a living room. A journal is a room of one's own, that private, quiet place we must have if we are to survive and grow. I do not invite guests into my journal, so I do not have to keep it neat and orderly and clean. I throw anything in it, in any form, never knowing what may turn out to be valuable. My journal is my place to let go of formal constraints, to be crazy and creative, to take off my masks, to be me, to find me.

As we free ourselves from the constraints of correctness, as we knock the critics off our shoulders, we gain greater energy and attention for the real writing-and-being process. We begin to evolve deeper insights, deeper seeing. In my journal writing, the more I let go of concerns about form and arriving at "answers," the more energy I have just to follow the river of my own being. I sometimes drift into a kind of flow-writing where words are moving out from within me and I am just watching. Often, as I do this, my feelings start to change; I feel a kind of lifting and lightening and opening up. It is hard to explain, but almost invariably I feel better and my words lead me closer to my real feelings and needs and away from what I have been trained to feel.

Here, for example, is a brief excerpt from one of my old journals:

11/5 Early Morning

Yesterday rolled by like a dream—filled with shadows and strong feelings—with little time to get to know them. I feel them within me now, pawing at me to attend to them. When I finally got home in the evening, S and J were there—but by then I was moving like the tin man and was not good company for anyone. Later, I took the mat and the Mexican blanket I bought in Sonora—why is it so comforting to me?—and went out in the backyard with my wolf-brother Cody and lay beneath the stars. I slept on and off, fitfully, and felt afraid and alone and watched the stars do their slow dance—and sometime further into the night it all got kind of mixed together—the sleeping and waking—and the stars moved down close to me—and Cody's wolf-ness was there sleeping near me—and all the mixed feelings of the day were kind of dancing with the stars around me. . . .

As you write, remember that your journal is a private place, a safe place, and that there you do not need to impress anyone with either your writing or your being. There is no need to pretend. You can make no "mistakes" in your journal. Your journal is a personal and intimate tool, and each person's journal, like each person, is unique in its ways and its unfolding.

Commitment

Years ago, when I first started keeping a journal—without guidance and following some faraway whisper in my heart—I wrote sporadically, making entries days and sometimes weeks apart. I was still trapped within the small picture of writing I had been taught, so I only wrote when I thought I had something to say—when some profound insight or idea became clear in my mind. That very seldom happened, so I very seldom wrote. I spent most of my time waiting.

Now, I write to find out what I have to say, and this is such a difference. I write every day. I write in cafes and coffee shops; I write on buses and airplanes; I write in forests and on mountains; I write in the morning and in the middle of the night. I am under no compulsion to be clever or insightful or even to make sense when I write. Now, I am free to write "trash," because there is no such thing as trash in my journal—because this is my private place where no critics are allowed. And almost always, when I write freely and without standards, I begin to see things more clearly; I feel better about myself.

The point is: For things to happen, you must write. In my classes and workshops, I suggest to beginning writers that they must make more than a casual commitment to their journals and to themselves. This, too, is a change from our usual procedure. Our society conditions us away from commitment and toward the glitter of things that happen fast and easy. Madison Avenue entices us away from the beauty of the path with promises of instant arrival. We can buy a body with steroids and implants, buy love with a Mercedes-Benz, buy happiness with drugs and alcohol. We are taught to disdain the path itself and are blinded to the flowers that bloom along it.

Your journal comes with no such easy promises. Rather, its label reads something like this: "A lifetime of hard work toward staying alive and saving yourself."

You enter the writing-and-being process with no illusions of instant riches or instant enlightenment or even of any kind of arrival, in the sense of being finished with the work. It is not a destination you seek so much as a way of being and becoming. It is a path with a heart. Once out of their boxes, the wonders of word and self and universe continue unfolding before you. You enter upon the path not to arrive but to see the wonders of the path itself.

Begin, then, with a serious commitment to this strange thing called your journal, with no great or false expectations, but with openness and acceptance. I suggest that beginning journal keepers make this commitment: I will spend at least a half-hour a day, at least five days a week, alone with my journal. I suggest keeping this commitment faithfully for five or six weeks, then assessing where you are with it and whether you want to continue. By that time, most journalers, if they have been true to their commitment, are hooked on the process and well on their way to being lifelong writers.

Should life sometimes interfere with your commitment, however, as life has a way of doing, do not be too hard on yourself. Just find your way back to your journal as soon as you can—and take time then to write about why you have been away. Do not feel guilty. Welcome yourself back to the pages of your journal by writing about what has kept you away and how you are feeling about it. And with that, you are back into your writing-and-being work.

The word "alone" is an important part of this commitment. In a society that is always calling us away from ourselves, always telling us the answers are "out there" somewhere, and always trying to sell us those answers, we can easily drift into a life where we spend no time alone, where we have no relationship with ourselves. The commitment to be alone with your journal, and yourself, means taking time with no friends, no children, no television, no radio, no distractions—only yourself and your words, your writing and your being.

At first, you may find spending a half-hour alone with yourself and your journal every day to be boring or even frightening. If you do, that would be a good thing to write about. If you are bored or frightened by being alone with yourself, do not judge that observation but take it as a sign that it is time to work on that relationship. Talk to yourself about it.

Take your commitment to the writing-and-being process seriously. Set aside a special time each day to be with yourself. Do it as deliberately as you would arrange time to be with a friend or lover. It is the most important relationship of your life. It determines all others.

If you were to spend a half-hour a day with your journal, even if you never wrote a word, just being alone in the silence would be healthy. But do open your journal, there in the silence that will gradually become sacred for you, and begin to talk to yourself. Speak to yourself as openly and honestly as you can. Speak from your feelings, from your heart. That is the way all friendships begin.

No Rules

As you write, remember that you are keeping a journal, not a diary or a log. In a diary or a log, you record the things and events of your life: "Today this happened and that happened." In a journal, you may record some events, but you will also push on to explore your inner relationship to those things. In a journal, you are not writing about the outward events of your life so much as about what you feel and see arising within you. That is where the power is; that is where the choices are; that is where the freedom lies. So, in your journal, ask yourself questions, explore how you feel, and look at what is going on inside of you.

In journal writing, the images and words you use, the interplay between language and psyche, help you keep going and help you see possibilities. The following list of images and simple how-to advice about journal writing will both get you started and nudge you along. Remember: These are not rules. This is not a logical, linear business. Writing in your journal is different from writing a research paper. This is "me-search" into unexplored territory. There is an element of mystery and wonder, an element of "entering the river."

- Find a special place to be alone and quiet. Sit with your journal open and just breathe deeply for a while. When you are ready, write what you are feeling.

- Talk to yourself in your journal. Get to know yourself. Go slowly. Go gently. Make your journaling a special time.

- Sometimes, it is good to start with the facts. But then move beyond the facts, always asking, "How do I feel about that? What is going on inside me?" Write how you feel about one thing that happened today or one thing on your mind, on your heart. Explore your relationships with these things of your life.

- Remember that your journal is a private, safe place. There is no need to pose or pretend. Be as emotionally honest with yourself as you can. Take off some of the masks you have been trained to wear.

- Own your feelings. Speak for yourself. Say "I."

- Use your journal as a garbage can. Discard your angers, your fears, your doubts, your frustrations by writing about them in your journal. This will lessen their power over you. You will feel better.

- Remember: No critics are allowed in your journal. You have no need to worry about spelling, neatness, margins, semicolons, and such. Your journal is for spontaneity and creativity and discovery.

- You do not know where the process will take you. Be like a child playing in the garden, building in the garage, rummaging in the attic. Stay open. Expect the unexpected.

- Experiment. Write at different times of the day—an hour before dawn, at high noon, at dusk. Find a special time that feels right. Write in different ways, using different pens or a stubby no. 2 pencil. Write in different places—in your bedroom, at the park, at the coffee shop.

- Remember: If you sit quietly with yourself for a half-hour and write nothing, the time will not be wasted.

- Do not try to write "answers" or the big "truth." Small truths, little insights, will be more helpful.

- Avoid making judgments. Avoid putting things (and people) into neat little boxes and categories. You are not writing to be done with it. You are writing to keep your mind open; there is always more to be learned.

- Look for images and metaphors that express what things seem like, how they feel to you. Go beyond the world of logic.

- You live in a prison, many prisons. We all live in prisons of one kind or another—of being the children of our parents, of being male or female, of our prejudices, of our cultural training. Write to make the great escape, to save yourself.

- Carry your journal like a camera. Collect careful little "word photos"—the child's face in the bus window, the morning moon above the rush-hour traffic, the people running from the rain. You will begin to see more than you ever saw before. And it will all become precious to you.

- Ideas and feelings and images come back. The process is more circular than linear. Let things repeat themselves. There may be more to learn. Something is probably being worked out beyond your full understanding.

- If you fear someone will read your journal, if you have written things you don't want others to discover because someone will be hurt, it is all right to tear things out and destroy them. But write them first.

- Stand back in your mind. Observe yourself. Listen to yourself. Write about yourself in the third person sometimes—as if you are watching someone else.

- Write freely in your journal without stopping or censoring or judging. Welcome the words that come in. Think of the words as gifts from beyond your small knowing, from your greater knowing.

- Always treat yourself with love.

- Wonder about the motion of love. Ultimately, this work is about love. Ultimately, it is spiritual work.

- Each time you open your journal, you begin again. You are born again.

Beginning the Journey

You have your journal, and you are underway on this journey of writing and being. If you are new at it and are feeling hesitant and unsure of what to do, don't worry. Just as you learn to swim by entering the water, so you learn to write by opening your journal.

Begin your journey by simply opening your journal, putting down the day's date (and perhaps the time of day and the place), and starting to write. You enter your journal not to explore what you know but to discover how you feel. At first, this talking to yourself about feelings may seem awkward and uncomfortable, something like meeting a stranger. But it will get easier as you do it and as you explore suggestions and techniques to help it happen.

The Explorations that follow here and at the end of each succeeding chapter are designed to help you with the real work, the work of entering the river of your own writing and being. Follow them carefully. Do them faithfully. As you do the Explorations again and again, they will continue to yield new ways of seeing and saying.

EXPLORATION

Where Are You Now? (Part 1 of 2)

Find an hour or so to be alone with yourself, a pen, and paper. You will be writing on loose paper, rather than in your journal, so you can seal these pages in an envelope. During this time, reflect on the following questions and write down whatever comes along for you.

Obviously, you could spend hours, days, a lifetime, writing about these questions. But for now, do not worry about them too much. Just be curious; start looking and wondering. These questions address issues that will be explored in greater detail as you continue in your daily journal writing. Do not try to write answers; just let the questions lead you. Wonder, wander, speculate. Ask yourself further questions. Assume that you do not know, that there is always more to be discovered, more to be seen.

Before you begin to write in your journal, take a few minutes to close your eyes and breathe and grow quiet and watchful. Then, when you are ready, just write freely whatever thoughts, feelings, memories, come along in relation to the following questions.

- **How are you feeling about yourself right now?** What things about yourself do you feel good about? What things about yourself do you feel unhappy about right now? In what ways do you feel yourself changing or wanting to change?

- **How does your past feel to you?** How much weight from the past do you feel you carry with you now? Does your past feel light or heavy? Where is the weight of the past coming from? What are you angry about from your past? What regrets do you have? What would you like to let go?

- **What do you value in your life now?** In what kinds of things do you find meaning, value, purpose? What matters? Who matters?

- **What are your dreams, goals, needs?** In what directions do you need to go with your life?

- **What are your spiritual beliefs now?** Can you articulate them? Have they changed over the years? What specific things in your life feel "spiritual" to you?

When you are finished with this writing-exploring, fold the pages like a letter, seal them in an envelope, and write your name on the outside. Put the envelope in a drawer where you can find it when you finish your current journal (or at the end of your class or group sessions). You can then read it—like a letter from someone you once knew—and reflect upon changes and growth in your writing and being.

EXPLORATION

Looking at Your Day

The four questions that follow can help beginning journal writers get a feel for some basic uses of the journal. You can use these questions at any time to help you attend to specific things in your life and look more closely at your day. You can think of these questions when writing alone or when working with a class or a writing group. You can focus in depth on just one question or ask yourself all of them. And you can respond to these questions again and again, because each of your days is unique.

To prepare for this journal writing, sit quietly, close your eyes, and breathe deeply for a few minutes.

- **In your mind, look back over your day.** (Or work with the previous day, if you are writing in the morning.) Beginning when you woke up, review the day. What were the feelings of the day? What were the happenings, subtle and overt, of the day? Who were the people of the day? For a little while, just watch yourself, your "selves," going through this day.

- **In your journal, respond to the following questions about your day:**

  - *When were you angry or frustrated?* Describe a specific time during your day when you felt angry or frustrated about something. What was going on? Who was involved? How did you respond? Where is your anger or frustration now? What did you do with it?

  - *When did you feel good?* Describe a small, good moment in your day—a specific time when you felt good about yourself, when you felt at ease or at one with yourself, when you felt "at home" in the world, when you smiled. Perhaps it was when you stepped out of your house in the morning and saw a fragment of the waning moon in the eastern sky just ahead of the sun. Or maybe it was when you came home after a long day and your cat purred for you. Or perhaps the moment came when a small, pleasant memory surfaced unexpectedly.

- *What would you change?* Maybe you would change a choice you made, something you did, or something you said during the day. Rewrite that moment in your journal the way you would have it unfold.

- *Who made your day better?* Describe specifically what someone else did that helped you and made your day go better. Look closely at what they did and how it changed your feelings. See it. Appreciate it. Value it. Thank them.

It may seem ironic, but these "looking-at-your-day" questions can help you to live more fully in the moment, to be here now, to be more alive. This kind of journal writing slows you down, helps you attend to life rather than rushing past it. Use these questions to keep yourself grounded in the days and moments of your life. Come back to them often in your journal work.

two

Entering the River

No one can enter the river wearing the garments of public and collective ideas. He must feel the water on his skin. He must know that immediacy is for naked minds only, and for the innocent.

—THOMAS MERTON, *RAIDS ON*
THE UNSPEAKABLE

The River

To begin to "write real," as my students sometimes call it (that is, to keep a journal and to write from our hearts and our feelings) is to enter the river of our writing and being. This is a different matter from standing on the bank of the river and studying writing, or writing strictly formal papers that are divorced from our feelings and our being.

There are two ways to know the river (and the "river" is anything, everything). One way to know the river is to stand upon the bank and measure and analyze it. The river is so many feet wide, so many feet deep, so many miles long. There are so many gallons of water per minute passing any given point. We could dip into the river with test tubes and analyze the constituents of the water. We could measure the temperature of the water. We could identify and label the creatures that live in the water. In this way, we could come to "know" the river—punch the data into our computers, carry a printout in our briefcases, become "experts." But this would be only one way of knowing the river, and a narrow and illusory way at that.

The great danger is that we might come to believe that the river we knew in the boxes of our minds was the "real" river, that we would separate ourselves from the real river, that we would have no dynamic relationship with the reality. Then the river would be dead for us, and we would be dead in relation to it. We would be incapable of seeing the real river or loving the river. We would be lost and bored behind our hard eyes and our expert minds.

And the river, remember, is anything, everything: It is our partner, our child, our mother, our father, our school, the house we live in, our job, the tree in our front yard, life itself.

But there is another way to know the river—a way that is not encouraged in our left-brained culture. This way seems frightening at first because it asks us to let go, to give up the need to control. Yet this way leads not to boredom but to life, and it can only be found with a beginner's mind. This way, of course, is to enter the river.

To know the river by entering it is different from standing on the bank and analyzing it. To know the river in this way is to step down off the bank, to enter the river, to feel its water upon our naked skin, to join the river, to become one with it. This way is difficult for us, for we have been taught to conquer and control the river, to dam (damn) the river, to kill it for profit. We have been taught that the river is our enemy. We have been led to believe that we have something to lose by entering the river.

A Memory

I am five years old. I am with my older cousins and my aunt and uncle. The Nebraska summer afternoon is hot and humid. We are going swimming in the river that flows through my uncle's farm. I have never swum in the river before.

We step down off the grassy pasture bank into the sand and ankle-deep water. The afternoon is sultry. The water feels cool and the sand tickles the bottoms of my feet. We cross some shallow-moving water to a sandbar, laughing and splashing, and then we start out into the channel. The current picks up, and the water comes to my knees and then to my waist. My cousins dash ahead, floundering and yelling as they fall into the moving water. (In the river, the water is always moving.)

I inch out very slowly, becoming concerned. This is a very different experience from being in the wading pool in town. This water is alive and dark and filled with mystery. It pulls at me and the sand keeps moving out from under my feet. And there is nothing to hold onto. The water moves up to my chest, and the bottom keeps drifting away. I am afraid. I imagine giant gray catfish with bulging eyes and sucking mouths waiting for me in the dark water. I am afraid. The water pulls at me and seems to want me to go with it. I look for my uncle then, and fasten to his arm. In a small voice, I tell him I want to go back to the bank. . . .

Since then, I have undergone a long training for life on the riverbank. Insurance and investments, they told me. Boxes and boundaries. But I have not lived on the riverbank very well.

Always within me has been that five-year-old boy who remembers. Who remembers the pull of the river. Who remembers the fear and the wonder of that channel, alive and turning and rolling, on and on. On to the Platte . . . and to the Missouri and the Mississippi . . . and on to the gulf and the ocean . . . and on . . . .

Now, each time I run with the sunrise and morning star, each time I sit in silence and breathe, each time I open my journal and pick up my pen, I am again stepping off that grassy pasture bank. . . . The water is inching up, tugging and laughing. . . .

And so it is with the intertwined river of our writing and being. We enter this river through our hearts, through our personal writing, through our journals.

The Process

Before we move to the details of keeping a journal, the ways to enter the river, it is helpful first to take a brief look at the whole writing process. This will help clarify the small way we have sometimes been trained to view and use our language. It will provide a sense of the greater possibilities that lie before and within us.

To do this, I have drawn a picture for you, my personal petroglyph, of a way to envision the whole writing process. As I have gradually entered the river of my writing and being and have tried to help others do the same, the writing process has come to feel something like this to me:

This wiggly little petroglyph is not how the writing process actually looks, of course. The process cannot be reduced to a logical, linear explanation. Thus, any picture of it, any "story" about it, will necessarily be inaccurate, untrue, and limiting. But some pictures, some stories, are more useful and healthier than others—because they admit they are only stories, and so they leave room for wonder. Too often, my writing teachers were experts (or thought they were supposed to be), and their stories about the writing process left little room for wondering, about either my writing or my being.

This little story-sketch of the writing process grew out of my doodling in my journal and my efforts to explain to other teachers and to my students how the writing process felt inside of me, how it felt when I entered it—when a feeling or memory or idea emerged from within me and found its way into my journal and then, sometimes, out of my journal and into a piece of public writing. The poet Robert Frost once said that the process of writing a poem begins as a lump in the throat, a sense of wrong, a homesickness, a lovesickness, and that these feelings eventually find the thought and the thought finds the words.

My students respond to my petroglyph-picture of the writing process because the squiggly part on the left reminds us that all writing (a poem, essay, letter, journal entry, whatever) comes from the same process, and that all effective and meaningful writing has its source not "out there" somewhere but within us.

That is precisely where our story-sketch of the writing process begins—within us, within our hearts, with our feelings, which are our first response to all experience:

The asterisk in the picture represents an emotion, a feeling within us. It represents our first, natural response to life. This is where the language-learning-growth process properly begins—in our hearts, not in rational, logical, analytical thought. Depending on the situation, the asterisk may represent anger, fear, doubt, confusion, joy, guilt, wonder, delight, or some other emotion. It is feeling—and feeling is, always, our first experience of the world.

So we must begin with our feelings. Feelings are where our words become flesh; they are the grounding of our writing and being. Our words, then, must be born in our hearts and find their way to our heads. In a technological society, we are too often taught to devalue and deny our feelings. But it is only through our hearts that we can enter the river, touch the world, and establish relationship. Without feeling, without the heart, our writing and our being too easily turn into artifice, image, pretense, games.

The simple act of starting with the heart can transform both our writing and our being. As we take back our feelings, value and validate them, acknowledge and explore them, we experience a new creativity and power in our words and a new vitality in our lives.

What we have been taught is true, of course: We are rational creatures. Eventually. But first, wonderfully first, we are feeling creatures. And if we do not begin in feeling, our rationality becomes a cold, dead, dangerous thing. It is a skeleton without a heart. So we must take back our hearts. This is the part of the writing process, and of our being, that we have so often been educated to ignore. When we take back our feelings, our words and our being come alive, and things are never the same again.

To enter the river of the writing process—and the process of our being—we must begin at the source: with our feelings. "No one," as Thomas Merton tells us, "can enter the river wearing the garments of public and collective ideas." We must feel the water on our own skin. Otherwise, our writing and our being become empty acts, disconnected from our hearts, from ourselves, from the earth. We must start by acknowledging that we are feeling creatures first and that our words, if they are to be strong and honest and effective, and if they are to lead us toward health and growth and insight, must begin with and acknowledge those feelings.

And our feelings do guide us, quite easily and naturally, as we give ourselves permission to feel and to express and to explore them with our words—as we do in a journal. Then we can see the full, living language process begin deep within us. It begins in a place beyond words and beyond the manipulations of teachers and tyrants. It begins even before it develops into language, as we know and use it. The language process begins in the whirl of images, memories, and feelings within us, and in the churning soup of our subconscious. It begins long before we are ready to think about outlines and paragraphs and even complete sentences. It begins as a subconscious circling of that ✱ of pain, grief, anger, or confusion. It begins in our natural inclination to deal with and survive and grow from our feeling response to the stuff of our lives.

So, this crude sketch of a feeling and our prelanguage response to it looks something like this:

feelings
imagery
dreams

Beneath and beyond our conscious, left-brained knowing, we circle our feelings with the prelanguage of our bodily knowing, with internal imagery, and with our dreams when the conscious mind is sleeping. When permitted and encouraged to do so, our psyche responds to our pain, confusion, and struggle with its natural instinct toward survival and health. Like an oyster encircling an intruding bit of sand, this process, if encouraged and aided, makes of our pain pearls of growth and learning. But if stifled and denied, as it so often is—because that is how we are trained—the bits of sand of our natural pain and struggle grow into great unacknowledged rocks and boulders that we are doomed to carry with us through life, the awful burden of our denial of feeling and our training to become rational creatures.

When the process of feeling is encouraged and supported, when we learn to attend to rather than to deny our feelings, we naturally become consciously aware of them, acknowledge them, and move them to our left brain where we can encircle and explore them with the language of our thinking even as we continue to feel them.

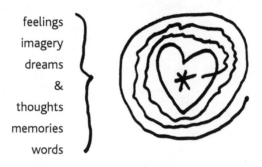

feelings
imagery
dreams
&
thoughts
memories
words

From this point on in the language process, our writing and being merge, and our words become tools to help us survive, for the next step is to allow this feeling-thinking to flow from us in the form of words on paper. This is the personal writing, or journaling, part of the process. In my sketch, it looks like this:

personal journal writing

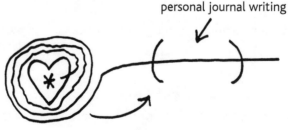

This next step into journal writing is the crucial part of the intertwined process of our writing and being. This is where we enter the river with our words. This is where we take back our feelings and learn to care. This is where we establish relationship—with ourselves and our words and the world. Then the frame begins to enlarge, and everything changes.

Personal writing in our journals is the heart of all our writing. There, our words become tools for our psychological, intellectual, and spiritual growth. There, too, our individual insights, feelings, memories, and stories become the source of all meaningful and effective public writing—gifts from our hearts to share with others.

The chapters that follow will return to this heart of the writing-and-being process, this personal journal writing, and explore how to make it work. But first it is necessary to complete the sketch of the whole writing process.

From the genesis of a journal, the writing process can move selected ideas, insights, feelings, observations—realizations that have emerged and begun to find shape and substance—out of our private writing and into the form and focus of a piece of public writing. Public writing is any writing that involves an audience beyond ourselves. It includes notes, letters, memos, instructions, essays, poems, stories, novels, editorials, and so on.

To complete my sketch, then, the entire writing process looks something like this:

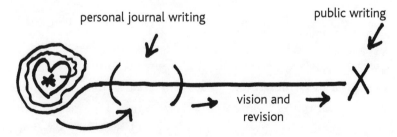

The final step, on the right, is writing that you ask others to read. Again, such a simple sketch does not begin to capture the complexity and mystery of the writing process. But even in its simplicity, it is more intricate than the picture most of us have been given through the traditional teaching of writing. As we explore the writing-and-being process, this sketch will help me talk about writing and will help you see the relationship between personal and public writing. The sketch will help us reclaim the gift and the power of our language.

Unlearning to Write

Looking at the writing process in terms of the sketch above, we can see that the process has often been presented to us in a small and truncated way. I was taught to write—and later, in turn, taught others to write—almost exclusively in terms of the public writing part of the process. With the picture of writing given by my teachers, this was my small vision:

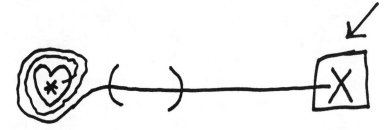

Few of my teachers said anything about the first part of the process, without which public writing, no matter how pretty or technically correct, is at best dead and at worst dangerous. No one said anything about where the "stuff" to write about came from. No one told me that the place to start was within myself or suggested that writing was, in itself, a way to discover things about myself and the world. I was taught to write when I had something (public) to say, so I seldom wrote. Now, I write in my journal to find out what I have to say—so I am forever writing.

For the most part, my teachers involved me only in the very end of the writing process. (This was not their fault—they taught as they had been taught and could not see the frame around the picture of their teaching.) And when I became a teacher, I did unto others what had been done unto me. I said to my students such absurd things as this: "I want from you a 500-word essay, due on Friday, on 'Capital Punishment.'" (Or "What I Did Last Summer" or "The Globe Theatre" or "Chaucer's Use of the Semicolon.") And, just as I had done as a student, they entered this whole magical, mystical, wonderful process unaware and just a few psychological/spiritual centimeters from the public "product" demanded by their teacher. Just as I had done, they began the process on the Thursday night before the product was due, on Friday morning. They filled some meaningless (to them) form with empty words, hoping to please their English teacher, get a good grade and pass the course, get the hell out of there, and never write again.

For my students, writing was, after all, only a subject in school—an exercise done for an English class. The audience was only an English teacher, waiting with his red pen. The writing came from nowhere and went nowhere. It had little relationship to the real lives of the writers or to their feelings or their struggles to survive and grow and find meaning in the world. They did not take it with them out the door and into their lives when they left my classroom. It did not help them to survive. It was too small, too meaningless, too dead. It did not have a heart.

And so, my students turned in their little products on Friday, and I, like the good writing teacher I had been trained to be, took them home and graded them on the weekend (usually on Sunday night, because I did not want to read these products any more than the students had wanted to write them). And of course, their writing was generally dull and boring and uninspired (how could it have been otherwise?). And of course, I carefully marked all of their errors, as I had been trained to do, and graded them accordingly. And of course, I sat in the teachers' lounge with my colleagues on Monday morning, lamenting how lazy and dumb my students were.

When I returned the papers to my students, they would look at their grades and then throw the papers into the wastebasket on the way out. Most of them were convinced not only that they could not write but that there was no reason they would want to write. Writing was mostly a game played in Nelson's English class.

When the first part of the writing process is missing, the last part has little meaning beyond a grade in school. Without the first part, without the living-beating-laughing-crying heart, nothing happens in the writing or in the writer. Nothing moves and changes. There is no life. The river does not flow.

The Entry

Start with your feelings. That is where you enter the river. If, when you sit with your journal, you find no strong emotions that need your immediate attention, then you can attend to other, subtler things. But learn to look closely. If feelings need your attention, especially "negative" feelings, there is great value in simply taking them out and putting them in your journal. For me, this is the immediate and fundamental use of my journal.

Sometimes, when I can't sleep at night because I am angry or worried or feeling overwhelmed by the stuff of my life, I get up, open my journal, and list what is bothering me. After doing this for a while, I feel myself relaxing, letting go. Almost invariably, I can then go back to bed and sleep.

So, say your anger—swear and scream in your journal. Say your hurt, your sorrow, your grief—cry in your journal. Say your fears—let your journal have them. When I use my journal in these ways, I almost immediately feel better somehow—as if I am a little less trapped or I have a little more room inside to breathe, a little more room for feelings of love for myself and others.

I sometimes refer to this kind of journal work as "taking out the garbage." Your life is like a house, the home of your being. If you do not take out the garbage, the house fills up with it. It becomes an unhealthy place to live. You cannot see out the windows. You see everything through the filter of your own garbage. You become sick and make unhealthy choices. And your garbage spills onto those around you.

But as you learn to use your journal to clean out the garbage, the things of your life begin to feel less polluted. Since nature always moves to fill a vacuum, when you take out your garbage and put it in your journal, something else moves to occupy that space within. That something else is always a little more positive than the garbage you took out, a little closer to where you need to be. No instant enlightenment. No lightning flashes. No miracles. But a slow movement begins toward the peace that lies at the center of your being.

Being trained to write what we think rather than what we feel is just one of the many ways we have been conditioned to deny our feelings. It takes hard work to reclaim them, sitting quietly with our journals and asking ourselves, "How do I feel about that?" And "that" can be any-thing—what the boss said to me today, the phone call from my mother, the argument with my friend, my father's alcoholism; the rainbow over the freeway on the way home. . . . When we start with our feelings, we are always engaged in discovery.

We never know exactly what we feel, because we never feel "exactly." So we are always exploring and wondering and learning, always getting to know ourselves—and the universe—a little better. This work goes beyond logical, linear thinking. When I ask myself how I feel about something, I am exploring my relationship to it—and it is always related to other things, and ultimately to everything. So while it may sometimes seem that you are working on trivial and mundane things in your journals, do not be fooled.

Human consciousness is a great and wondrous thing. We do not know where it ends. It may well be that we can follow the ripples outward forever from that "small" thing, from that event dropped like a pebble into the ocean of our consciousness. It may be that if we learn how to follow these ripples, the things of our lives will lead us through ripples of relationship outward to wisdom and love.

EXPLORATION

Fists into Flowers

Much of your early work in the journal will involve going back into your past, into your childhood. Like the rest of us, you are, to some degree, a "victim" of your parents' inadequate love and the wounds of your childhood. You still have within you pain, loss, and anger from your childhood.

You grew up in a society that taught you to devalue your emotions. Within that society, you may have been raised in a dysfunctional and wounded family where you also learned to deny your feelings. There is much work to do in your journal to free yourself from the past so you can be here now. You may wonder, "Why should I want to go back to those feelings? That is the last thing I would want to do." But if it is painful, it is not healed. If it is not healed, you will never be done with it. This Exploration will help you begin to go back and heal your life.

Find a quiet place where you will not be interrupted. Sit quietly with your journal beside you. Sit with your spine straight and your body relaxed. In the background, perhaps some soft music . . . .

• **Breathe deeply, fully.** Feel your body relaxing, letting go. For just a while, attend only to your breathing. For just a while, do not worry about anything. Right now, give yourself permission to be concerned only with your breathing. Quietly watch your breath come and go. Feel its miraculous rhythm. Feel your body relaxing into your breathing. For about five minutes, just breathe. Each time your mind wanders away from your breathing, which it will, bring it gently back to the ebb and flow of your breath.

- **Look within for what feels like a fist, tight and clenched.** Your "fist" may be something immediate: a test you are worried about, an argument you had yesterday, a feeling of anxiety about something you must do. Or it may be a fist you have been carrying inside you for a long time: a chronic tightness from old anger at your father, a "holding on" to the pain of a long-ago lost love, a general frustration with your job.

- **Write about it in your journal.** Begin to let go of this clenched fist by putting your feelings in your journal. As you do this, do not write answers, do not analyze, do not judge. Only see and say. In gentleness, take the tightness out of your inner feelings and put it in your journal as best you can at this time. Do this for about five minutes, writing steadily, writing whatever comes to you in relation to the fist you are focusing on.

- **Focus again on your breathing.** See if your breathing is a little easier now. See if you seem to have a bit more room inside for your breathing and your being. See if the fist has begun to open just a little, to let go. It may be that the fist feels even tighter now— because you have brought it more fully to the surface of your consciousness. That is all right. Whatever is happening is part of your natural healing process. Just breathe for another five minutes or so.

- **Return to your journal and write again.** Once again, write steadily and freely for another five minutes or so, pouring out whatever needs to come. Some fists open easily and are quickly gone. Others, when they open, release a torrent of strong feelings they have been clutching. Whatever happens for you, watch it and stay with it. Go back and forth, from your writing to your breathing, as many times as you need in relation to this particular fist. If you tire, leave it and come back another day.

Your journal and your breathing, your writing and your being, work hand in hand, each helping the other. Use this exercise often, in relation to specific issues and simply as a regular writing-relaxation exercise. As you do it, you will notice your writing and your breathing and your being becoming lighter and freer.

EXPLORATION

The River of Your Life

This Exploration will give you a feel for the flow, the movement, of your life that has brought you to where you are now. It will help you to begin making friends with your life. The first time you do this Exploration, don't do too much. Don't let it overwhelm you. You can always come back in the quiet of your journal and look again.

Find quiet time once again and settle yourself with your journal at hand. Once again, begin by just sitting and breathing gently for awhile. . . .

• **Look back over the "river" of your life.** In your mind's eye, fly over the river of your life. Follow it back to its source, to your birth. Look at that time. Wonder about it, about where you came from, about your parents, about your conception, about the miracle of your birth.

- **Take up your journal and write freely about your birth.** Let the words flow from you—questions, wonderments, facts, feelings. Where were you born? What was the season of the year? Who was there? What must your mother have been feeling? Your father? What was it like to come from that nine-month meditation in your mother's womb and into the world? Can you feel any distant memories, any whispers? Let your words flow from you, dreaming how it must have been.

- **Close your eyes and follow further the river of your life.** Follow it from its source, from your birth, along its course over the first ten years or so of your life. Where did it flow smoothly? Where were there rapids and rough water? What was going on outwardly—moves, changes, losses, relationships? And what was going on inwardly? What were your fears, your struggles, your joys?

- **Write about the first ten years of your life.** Put down bits and pieces as they come to you—memories, feelings, images, fragments of scenes from the flow of your life then and the stream of your consciousness now. Just write and let the feelings flow for several minutes. Remember that whatever comes up is all right. Do not judge it; just put it down. Do not worry about proper chronology or facts; just gather moments and feelings and insights until the flow slows or until you tire.

- **Breathe again and follow your life further in your mind.** Watch for places where it flowed smoothly. Watch for rough water or abrupt changes of course. What caused those changes—loss, death, separation, moves, other changes? Notice who was there with you and what was happening in those relationships. Just breathe and watch and feel.

- **Take up your journal once more and write again.**

You get the idea. Keep doing this until you have followed the river of your life up to now, but not to the point of becoming overwhelmed. You can always go back and fly over the river again in this same way and see more and feel more. And each time you do this Exploration, as you look back and write, your feelings about your life will change. The river will become more dear to you, more beautiful. Thus, you can use this gift of language to heal your wounds, to let go of your anger, to take out the garbage. In this way, you write to free yourself from your past so you can find peace in the present.

three

Seeking Silence

Valuing Empty Spaces

Just as music depends for its meaning upon the empty spaces between the notes, our words must have silence around them or they, too, lose their meaning. If I do not seek quietness around me, I cannot hear the words that my heart whispers. And if I do not seek silence within, I will never know the power of my words as instruments of creation. But it is hard to find silence out there these days—and even harder to find the silence within.

Recently, I gave my class a writing-and-being Exploration. The assignment was simply to select a quiet place and "be with the sunset." The challenge was to sit quietly with their journals nearby and just breathe and be with the sun as it disappeared behind the turning edge of the Earth—and then, when the sun was gone, to reflect for a while in their journals.

As always, I did the assignment along with my class, and this is what I shared with the class the next week:

Somewhere the Sun Is Setting

I had planned to go find the sunset this evening. I had planned to put my journal and a bottle of water in my backpack, get on my bike, and make the long, hard pull to the top of South Mountain. I had planned to find a quiet spot there and sit with my back against a rock, facing west into the lowering sun. I had planned to close my eyes and breathe deeply, focusing only on the coming and going of my breath until my insides gradually grew still, until the muscles of my jaw relaxed and my brow smoothed and my eyes softened—until the evening began to breathe me. . . .

But this day had its way with my plans, and I didn't get there. And now I sit here weary at my computer. Willow-Cat is sleeping on my desk nearby. Somewhere, in another room, Springsteen is singing, "I'm on fire." And somewhere, out there, the sun is on fire. Somewhere beyond my bedroom window and the garden wall, beyond the oleander bushes and the asphalt-shingled roofs and the TV antennas, beyond the drone of the evening news and the roar of the rush-hour traffic, the sun blazes silently above the blue Estrella Mountains . . . and I am not there.

Conspiring Against Noise

It seems such a simple thing to be still and then to write the words that come from the silence. But the world and its noise are too much with us, and we struggle to find the stillness. As we become writers, we carry our journals with us everywhere. We learn to steal bits of time to write on crowded buses, in noisy restaurants, in droning meetings. Amid the sound and the hurry of our days, we sneak a few minutes here and there to jot down memories and insights and feelings; we record bits and pieces to pick up later. And that is good; I do it all the time. But I know my writing and being cannot live and grow on such moments alone.

As I write this, I am home alone on a Sunday morning. I have had some tea. I have sat in silence for awhile and watched my breath come and go. No sound is in the house this morning, except for the occasional humming of the refrigerator and sighing of the sleeping dogs. Outside, the sparrows chatter distantly at the bird feeder. The wind plays the chimes on the back porch and rustles the leaves of the eucalyptus tree. This morning, because I am quiet, I can hear the wind. I can feel it nudging the long Arizona summer southward and bringing a hint of the changing seasons. Because I am quiet, I can feel my connections to this tilting planet.

But most days I do not have the luxury of this quiet morning that has come like a gift to me. So, we who do this writing-and-being work must take up our journals daily and seek silence like a lover. We must be deliberate. We must conspire against the forces of noise. On most days, my regimen of seeking silence goes something like this:

Quiet Place. At work, I get to my office early while the building is still quiet. I close the door, lock it, and unplug the phone, so I won't be disturbed. My office is small, but there is room to make a sitting pad in the middle of the floor with my old Mexican blanket. So my mind won't worry about the clock, I set my food timer for fifteen or twenty minutes and stick it in a drawer where I cannot hear its ticking, but its gentle ding will tell me when the time is up. Sometimes I light a candle to put on the floor in front of me.

Quiet Body. I fold my blanket so it is about four inches high, for a pad beneath my buttocks. I take off my shoes and settle into a half-lotus position with my spine straight and my hands resting on my knees. (This can be done as well by sitting in a straight chair with your feet flat upon the floor, your spine erect, your hands resting on your knees. The important thing is for the body to be relaxed yet alert—so sit as if your spine were suspended from the ceiling, and let the rest of your body relax and be supported by your spine.) I close my eyes and breathe deeply and fully for a few minutes, getting my body settled and comfortable.

Quiet Mind. Then I let my breath come and go naturally, easily, peacefully. I focus my mind on the coming and going of my breath. For this brief time, I give myself permission to be at rest in the universe, to be responsible only for attending to the wonder of my breathing. Inevitably, my mind wanders and worries and frets—but when it does I bring it, like a wayward child, back home to my breathing, gently and without judgment. That is all. So simple—and yet so hard. Some days it goes well, and I gradually settle in toward the center, toward the silence of just breathing. Some days my mind chatters and runs away no matter how many times I bring it back. But that is all right. There is no right or wrong to this—only the doing. Always, however it goes, my writing and my being are better for having had this time.

Quiet Journal Writing. When the timer goes off, I gently open my eyes. Then I set the timer for another fifteen minutes or so, turn to my journal, and write freely whatever words want to come from this quiet time that has taken me a little closer to my heart. When I read back over my journals, the words from these writing times almost always stand out as being simpler and stronger and more peaceful.

In a past journal, for example, I find this passage:

> this morning the room is soft and gentle—it welcomes me with sighs of early sunlight—i breathe and stretch and settle in and very soon the center, the silence, is with me. now, as i write, i am reminded of ric's poem about the homesick snail sliding down its silver track, "looking for the very thing/it carries on its back." that fits so well for me, for this breathing/writing/going-in process—it is all here—in me—or it is nowhere . . . and today i find it once again, enter once again into the fringe of that holy place—but just the fringe is enough, enough for now, enough to keep me going this day, this lifetime, perhaps . . . and i know i will leave this room and wander from that fringe again, into the sound and the fury—but having been near that holy place, i will remember and i will find my way back—because it is the only home there is—the only home i need. . . .

If we wish to tap the true power of the writing-and-being process, we must make time each day to seek silence, to be still and know. Set aside such times deliberately, faithfully, and hold to them against the roaring world.

Writing to Share

From here on, the Explorations in each chapter will have a dimension called "Toward Public Writing." The previous chapter looked at the whole writing-and-being process with its beginnings in the feelings in our hearts; its movement out and into the personal writing of our journals; and, ultimately, the movement of some of this writing into public writing to be shared with others. Once your writing is grounded in its source—your heart and your journal work—once you begin to find the beauty of your own voice and the power of your own stories, you may feel a natural urge to share your writing with others.

While the Explorations that follow are always grounded in journal writing, we will also look at ways to turn the discoveries of our personal writing into meaningful public writing. This is the natural movement of all writing, the way of all effective public writers. Even if you think you are solely a journal writer, I encourage you to work on the public writings, too—you may surprise yourself and, in working to tell your stories to others, you will continue to learn more from the stories yourself. If you are also an aspiring public writer, you will find that effective public writing flows naturally and powerfully from your journal work. And if you are a teacher trying to help your students toward articulateness in public writing, you will be amazed at what they begin to do once their public writing connects with their hearts.

In the "Toward Public Writing" suggestions, you will be encouraged to move some of your journal writing into another, more public dimension. As you work your words into effective writing for others, you need to be concerned about form and mechanics and punctuation, those things I told you not to worry about in your journal work. But now you have something to say, stories to tell, moments to show others. With each public writing piece you work on, you will discover elements of effective public writing—even as you continue to discover more about yourself.

The challenge in each of the public writings is to focus on some particular thing that has emerged from the jumble of stuff that has flowed into your journal, and then to give it form and make it sing. You will choose a focus, decide how to address your audience, decide what tone to use, and determine what to do with yourself as speaker. And of course, you will also try to do impossible things with your words—to somehow convey to another person the amazing, ineffable, contradictory, and complex world as you see it and feel it at this moment.

Yes, public writing is complex work. But don't be like the centipede that walked easily and naturally until someone asked it how it could do that with all those legs, and then it fell over in a heap. Rather, just stay with the heart of your writing, your own heart, your own feelings, your own honest words. Keep your words grounded in the simple honesty of speaking from your heart. The rest will happen naturally as you keep writing and working.

EXPLORATION

Exploring Your Epigraph

An epigraph (not to be confused with an *epitaph*, words on a gravestone) is a short quotation placed at the beginning of a piece of writing—a book or a chapter or an essay or, in this case, a journal—to set a tone for what will follow. I like using epigraphs in my writing. They give me a feeling of fellowship and support in my writing-and-being work.

For this Exploration, first find an epigraph (or, better yet, let an epigraph find you) to put at the beginning of your journal. The quotation you select for your epigraph can come from anywhere— the whole world of words is your hunting ground, from the Bible or the Koran or the Bhagavad Gita to a song or the label on a soup can. Or a child might utter something that you will recognize as your epigraph. All that matters is that it feels fitting, supportive, and encouraging for your life and feelings now, and for the journal where you are working on your writing and being.

Find quiet time and begin by sitting and breathing for a while with your journal by your side.

- **Write your epigraph at the top of a page in your journal.** Read it softly to yourself a few times, savoring the words, feeling them. Then close your eyes and breathe, and be still for a few minutes. Feel the words of your epigraph still flowing through you without worrying about what they mean.

- **Open your eyes and write whatever comes to you in relation to your epigraph.** Wonder as you write. Wonder about how your life feels now and how your epigraph points to some of that feeling. Look beneath the surface of your life. Use your writing to discover more, to see more. Speculate. Imagine. Fantasize. Play with your words, remembering always that you do not know what you know until you see what you say.

Toward Public Writing

After you have wandered and wondered and explored in your journal, think about sharing with someone else your epigraph and something that has emerged for you in relation to it.

Go over the material you have written in your journal and find something you would like to share with others. Focus on some small, specific thing—a memory that came up as you worked with your epigraph, a discovery that surprised you, something you struggled with, or an insight you want to share—something you feel would be interesting or valuable or helpful to others.

Work on it further in your journal, or move it onto separate paper or into your word processor, however you work best as you move toward public writing. Do not take on too much material.

Think in small, careful terms. Let this small piece grow and emerge, and see what happens.

As you work, keep in mind this warning: The danger with this Exploration is the temptation to write the "truth"—to generalize or lecture or preach about your epigraph. Don't give into that temptation—it leads to sloppy thinking and boring writing. This is a danger to avoid in all of your writing.

Keep your seeing and your saying alive by staying grounded in "real stuff" as you write.

This "real stuff" is a crucial concept for us writers—it is what good writing teachers often refer to as the difference between "showing" and "telling." Powerful, meaningful writing is almost always big on showing and small on telling. The difference between showing and telling, for example, is the difference between a story about your mother's awakening in the recovery room after surgery and being concerned about your need to get some rest versus a Mother's Day card filled with generic words about "a mother's love." One shows the love, grounds it in story, in real stuff. The other only tells about the love, only uses the abstract word. One is alive and real. The other is weak and lifeless.

In effect, this Exploration asks you to take a "telling" (a quotation or epigraph) and turn it into a "showing," a story that grounds the quotation or epigraph in the real stuff of your life. So, in this Exploration, as in all of your writing, work to create a piece of public writing in which you share something particular, something real. Let it take whatever form emerges as you work. Trust the process. There is no right or wrong—only learning and growing.

Here is a piece, for example, that found its way, after much writing and rewriting, out of my journal and into public writing. I had given this assignment to one of my undergraduate writing classes at ASU—and then (since I always do the writing I ask my students to do) I went back to some of my favorite quotations. I quickly settled on one that tugged at my heart, wrote it at the top of a page in my journal and let the memories flow. Eventually, I shared this piece with the class:

Teachers

The quotation I selected for my journal epigraph is an old Buddhist saying that goes something like this: "When the student is ready, the teacher will come." Years ago, when I first heard it, I thought the idea was mildly intriguing—but I didn't believe it was true. After all, the world was a machine that operated on logic and cause and effect, and I was merely a smaller machine that operated on stimulus and response. There was no room in this world for such quaintness from some antique and irrational culture. Since then, however, my eyes have opened a bit more, and I can see a little beyond my narrow training—I can see that such a truth has indeed operated in my life. The "special children" are a case in point. They came along when I needed them, when I was ready for them. They taught me well. They changed my life.

On the surface, it looked as if I quit teaching high school and moved to Lincoln with my wife and two small daughters so I could go to graduate school at the University of Nebraska. On the surface, it looked as if getting a doctorate was to be my education. But I know now that my real teachers showed up late one September afternoon. Eight of them. They came to live with us. They were labeled "trainable mentally retarded." They were slit-eyed and slobbering, gangling and gauche—and beautiful beyond my small seeing.

The children taught me well, and I was ready for their teachings. They taught me how to change beds and change diapers and change my life. When I came home in the afternoons, they taught me not to worry too much about tests and sonnets and semicolons; they taught me about crayons and cartoons and laughing and crying.

For four years, in this way, they taught me, until I could see their beauty, until I loved them like my own. They changed my life—and then they left me to live their lessons on my own.

EXPLORATION

Reflections on Your Name

As we will see again and again, doing this writing-and-being work we are always, aware of it or not, exploring the crucial questions "Who am I?" and "What matters?" Exploring and telling stories about our names pulls us into exploring who we are and where we came from. (Note: This is also a helpful Exploration to do early on if you are in a writing class or group, as it will help you to learn and to remember each others' names.)

To begin, open your journal to a clean page, take a few deep breaths and get quiet.

- **Write your full name across the top of the page.** Look carefully at those combinations of letters, those words that somehow identify you. Think about where those names came from and where you came from, and think about all the memories and feelings and stories connected to your full name.

- **Begin to write, freely and openly, anything that comes to your mind and heart in relation to your names.** Wander and wonder about your names—about nicknames you might have been called, about names you might have wished for, about how your names may have changed as you grew older or got married. Wonder about your names as symbol, as sound. How do your names feel to you? How have your feelings about your names changed? Think about your parents, your ancestors, the generations who came before you. What of them is in your names? Who named you? How did they pick the names they gave you? If you could rename yourself now, what would you choose? Think of specific moments, memories, stories that somehow involve your names.

- **Write in your journal without thought for form or correctness.** Write to collect the many thoughts and feeling and memories within you—in relation to you, your name, your being.

- **Go away when you tire.** Come back later and read what you have written and write more.

Toward Public Writing

There, in the pages of your journal, you now have the seeds of many pieces of public writing—stories, poems, essays, whatever.

For now, pick one particular story, memory, incident, or feeling that has emerged for you in your writing up to this point. Focus on that in your journal, and free-write again, getting down whatever comes to your mind and heart in this more detailed exploring.

Let it take a form, a "shape" on the page—a poem, a short narrative, a "memory-story," an essay, a letter to someone about your name, whatever feels fitting for what you have to say. Begin molding it into a public piece. Work on it. Go away from it for a while. Come back and read it aloud to yourself; add to it and make changes. Do this over and over until it emerges and begins to feel right. Give it a title and perhaps even an epigraph. Proofread it, and get it ready to go out into the world. Like all real writing, if you have done your work well, it will have taught you much about your writing and your being—and it will be meaningful and helpful for others.

Here is a name-writing piece that my friend and fellow writer Fortino did awhile back when we were writing together in a workshop:

My Name

The first day of eighth grade, I hid from you
By approaching my first-hour shop teacher before he took roll,
Asking, begging this burly man if he would call me Tino
Instead of reading my entire birth name:
Fortino Martinez Gomez.

At twenty-seven, I don't hide from you anymore.
I understand you better now.

Fortino was my dad's first name,
As well as his dad's and his dad's.
It's a Mexican first-born male tradition
That will stop with me:
A bad temper is nothing to give away.

Martinez was my mother's idea,
And I love her for it.
It was her maiden name that she didn't want to let go,
Even though marriage is one step closer to Catholic heaven.
She gave it to me

So that we will remember who we are
And who she used to be.

My grandfather, Grandpa Martinez, was a copper miner
With the nickname of Mono,
Which means "big monkey" in Spanish.
He lied about his age to start working at thirteen—
Drilled for copper,
Drank whiskey like water,
And blasted underground tunnels,
Digging the earth for pennies.
So, Martinez, my middle name, my mother's gift,
Often brings me inspiration
To work hard for sometimes nothing.

Gomez is a last name that came from a grandfather I never knew.
My grandmother ran from him, never looking back.
I've heard stories, but I can't accept them
Because I have seen what they have done to my father,
Fortino, Sr.,
The man without a father, who married my mother,
And gave me the name that I no longer hide from.

And Cornelia, a student from Germany who came to spend a year writing with me, wrote this touching poem about the nickname her mother called her as a child:

Munkel

Munkel
is what my mother called me when I was a child—
and it is what she still calls me

sometimes,
now that I am not a child anymore
Munkel
is a name that didn't exist until my mother created it

Munkel
sounds like a whisper like water like waves
and smells like damp earth
Munkel
is a fairy tale creature
Munkel
is a child hiding under a blanket
her mother coming in
laughing
I can see you—your hair is showing.

there are people I would like to call
Munkel
and I'm sad that I don't

but at night
when I can't sleep
I can hear my mother calling me
dark and soft
Munkel.

Cornelia was writing in her second language of English, yet still she wove this beautiful memory with her careful words—a memory of her mother's nickname for her. Like Fortino, she wove this poem from the stuff of her life, from her history. You, too, have such stories connected with your names. Find them as you write quietly in your journal and remember. And then turn them into artifacts from your life to share with others.

EXPLORATION

Collecting Small Joys

Unless you are careful and deliberate, our society, with its blaring media and relentless marketing of entertainment, will dull you with its noise and pull you away from yourself. Unless you work deliberately to save yourself, you can easily just keep turning the volume up a little louder, watching another show, taking another pill, having another drink—and dying a bit more each day. In your journal writing, you are working in the other direction. You are working back toward the peace within your own heart. This Exploration will help you to refine your sensitivity, to sharpen your awareness, to live more fully in the precious moments of your life.

Begin by sitting quietly with your journal by your side. Breathe deeply and fully for a few minutes. Feel your awareness moving toward that quiet place in the center of your being. Just breathe.

- **In your mind, look back over your day for small joys.** Look for moments of meaning from your day—not logical, practical meaning but a deeper, quieter meaning. Seek moments that may have touched you so softly that you hardly knew it at the time.

- **In your journal, write about one of those moments.** Reach out tentatively with your words and pick up a moment—perhaps the half-remembered play of breeze and sun on your face as you walked to class this morning, the face of an old woman on the street, the almost forgotten brief touch of a friend's hand. Look at the moment carefully with your words. Watch yourself having that moment. Live it again, more fully, in your journal.

- **Reach out with your words and pick up another small moment of joy.** Find several from your day, always feeling for the preciousness at the heart of each moment.

Initially, this Exploration may be difficult. It is a bit like stalking wild mushrooms in the forest: At first, you think there are none anywhere, but then you find one—and then another. And suddenly they are everywhere, and you are amazed that you could not see them before.

That is the way this work goes: The more small joys you find, the more there are and the more you have. You become more attuned to these moments, to seeing and appreciating them even as they take place. You and your writing and the very quality of your life change.

Toward Public Writing

Go back to the small joys you have collected in your journal. Pick out one or two that you would like to share with others.

Turn these moments into small pieces of public writing, capturing, with your word choice and imagery, the heart of each moment. Think of creating small, precise pieces of seventy-five to a hundred words. But do not be tied to that limit; always listen to the piece itself, and let it become what it needs to become.

Make it clean and strong, a bit like haiku, with no wasted words. Communicate by showing, by dramatizing, not by telling.

By the words and the images that you use, by the experiences you show, let readers feel the moment for themselves.

Suzanne, for example, looked back into her journal and her life and found this moment, which she then worked into a gift to us through her careful words:

Pansy Water

Waiting for her to get ready, I lie on the bed, my coat still on. The overhead light is glaring down—too bright. It's so quiet. I feel heavy, tired. What a day. And more to be done. I need to get going.

I catch the movement of the closet door out of the corner of my eye. A smooth white cat peers out. One blue eye, one green. A pink bunny rabbit nose. He stares intently at something on the bedside table. Following his gaze, I notice a short glass vase filled with pansies. How did I miss them? Such intense color. Deep purple velvet with sunny yellow centers.

Ignoring me, the cat stretches and silently jumps on the bed, walking over my chest and onto the table. Gently, he pushes his face into the velvety bouquet. Purple petals, yellow centers, green stems fall to the table in disarray, framing the white face pressed into the clear vase—eyes closed, pink tongue making soft noises, lapping water. Pansy water.

My mind is no longer on the day and the things to be done. I feel light. Renewed by a smooth white cat with a penchant for pansy water.

Suzanne's piece is simple and powerful, like a painting. There is almost no telling—instead it shows the real stuff of her life. Her words take us there. We share her experience through her words.

Her story has a natural sense of form—beginning and ending with the words "pansy water" and focusing carefully on one small, exquisite moment.

four

Letting Go

The true purpose is to see things as they are . . . and to let everything go as it goes.

—Shunryu Suzuki, *Zen Mind, Beginner's Mind*

Shedding Hard Eyes

To enter the river of our writing and being, we need to shed the certainty and the arrogance and hubris of our hard-eyed training. Among the few "rules" in my writing classes are these: that students must leave their egos at the door, that they have soft eyes and a beginner's mind, that they let go and just watch and learn. These are not easy challenges to meet.

In *The Dragons of Eden*, Carl Sagan tells a creation story that helps put things in perspective and restore a sense of wonder—it comes from the astronomers. Fifteen billion or so years ago, the astronomers say, the universe was created in a cataclysmic explosion (the Big Bang Theory). To illustrate major events in the history of this still exploding-expanding universe, Sagan presents those fifteen billion years on the scale of a single year, beginning in January and ending in December. Into that compressed and metaphoric timeline, he plugs some well-known universal or historic happenings. As Sagan points out, the construction of such a calendar is inevitably humbling.

On a one-year scale, the Earth itself does not even condense out of interstellar matter until early September. Dinosaurs emerge on Christmas Eve. Flowers arrive on December 28. And the first humans do not appear until New Year's Eve, December 31—at 10:30 P.M. We have only been part of the picture for an hour and a half—ninety minutes.

Such a perspective should certainly restore in us a sense of wonder. Yet the narrow left-brained spectrum of "knowing," so emphasized over the last 300 years, has left us with the deadly illusion that we now know about all there is to know. This narrow perspective has given us television, cars, computers, space travel, and "smart bombs"—and has led us to believe that these are what life is all about. Such narrow knowing can make us arrogant. It can rob us of the necessary sense of mystery, wonder, and reverence, without which we will lose the meaning of our lives and destroy our Mother Earth.

Sagan observes that all of humanity's recorded history occupies only the last ten seconds of December 31, and the centuries from the Middle Ages to the present take up little more than one second. He has arranged his one-year metaphor so that the first cosmic year has just ended. Yet, he suggests, despite the insignificance of the instant we human creatures have existed in cosmic time, what happens on Earth at the beginning of the second cosmic year will depend largely on the scientific wisdom and "the distinctly human sensitivity" of humanity.

We are now poised precariously at the beginning of this second cosmic year. If we are to survive and continue, if we are to fulfill a fraction of our potential, individually and collectively, we must shed the hard eyes and arrogance of the tiny, scientific age of certainty through which we have just passed. That is why we do this journal writing—taking life out of boxes, letting go of judgment, taking back wonder, and, in the process, rediscovering our distinctly human sensitivity and letting it be our guide. This is the knowing we need to keep in our minds and hearts as we continue to explore the writing-and-being process.

Seeing with Soft Eyes

Writing in our journals invites us to practice the art of just watching, of seeing things as they are. We practice soft eyes and beginner's mind. We refrain from making judgments as we write. We resist the need to arrive at solutions, answers. Rather, in our journal work we watch carefully, full of care for ourselves and for the process. We let go of the preconceived labels and boxes in our left brains. We look closely with our words, working to see as clearly and cleanly as possible.

From earliest childhood, we have been taught to judge ourselves and others and the world around us—to use words to file and box and categorize and label. We learn to do this so we can defend ourselves and control our world. So when we begin working in our journals, it is difficult to resist this training and to free ourselves just to see.

For example, suppose I write in my journal, "Today, I am feeling some strong anger toward my father." It is difficult then not to do as I have been trained, as my mind has been taught to do automatically, which is to attach a judgment of some kind: "and I shouldn't feel that way" or "and that is wrong" or "and he certainly deserves it." Such judgments kill the discovery process by sending us scurrying away from that feeling because it is "wrong" or because we are "not supposed to" feel that way. Or because, having judged it, having boxed it up and labeled it, we believe there is nothing more to see or say.

Judging and labeling leave us holding onto things. They prevent us from taking out our garbage. Then the garbage sticks to our fingers, our minds, our hearts, and we cannot let go of it. We walk out to the dumpster with our garbage, but we bring it back into the house with us. Much of the power of the journal process is in its potential to help us let go of our garbage and lighten our load. (That part of the process will be described in the next chapter.)

When we write, we need to stay open to our feelings, to follow them and learn from them. When writing about anger, for example, we can stay open and follow our feelings inward with our words: "I am feeling deep anger at my father today. When he called and said he wouldn't be able to come for Christmas, I didn't believe him—I felt angry—but beneath the anger, I feel hurt—and unloved—again, again—and I remember those same old feelings—I remember when I was ten years old and he didn't come to my Christmas program at school. . . ." Then we go on to tell that story in the journal, to let the hurt child tell that story and all the other stories, to heal those wounds. We tell our stories first in anger, then in letting go, and finally in love—the freeing love for our fathers and for ourselves.

Just as we let go of standards of language correctness in our journals, we also learn to let go of rules for our feelings. Feelings are just feelings, neither good nor bad. They come and go through us. What we do with those feelings, how we act upon them, is quite another matter, but the feelings themselves are just feelings. What we do with them—and what they do to us—has much to do with whether or not we follow them to their sources, stay open to them, let them be heard, let them tell their stories, and, ultimately, let them go.

So, in our journal work, we are continually practicing openness and wonder. It is not easy to overcome all those years of training to judge, evaluate, analyze, and categorize. When we catch ourselves following the old rules in our journals, it is a chance to practice. Rather than judging

("I see that I am judging, and I should not do that"), we can observe ("I see that I am judging when I say that") and let it be. All we need to do is see cleanly. Having seen, our being will do what needs to be done.

As we let go of the need to judge and begin just to see and say, the world slowly opens like a blossom for us. As the boxes in our minds fall away, the real world comes alive. As William Blake once observed, "If the doors of perception were cleansed, everything would appear as it is, infinite." For most of us, this happens very gradually, of course. It takes years, lifetimes. But it begins with the way we see and the way we say—and each works on the other. It begins in the journal, where we work on seeing and saying more clearly. As we write in our journals, we may think that we are only working on mundane little problems. Yet, invariably, we are moving along a spiritual path and the world inside us and outside us is changing, opening, blossoming.

Seeing and Saying

To use our journals to discover new ways to see the world and to say what we feel, we need to be aware that there are two general and very different ways of using our words. And the way we use our words makes a great difference in both our writing and our being.

We have generally been trained to use our words as if they were the things they name, as if they contained the reality of the things at which they can only point. When we use language in this way, our words take what we initially see and freeze what is not frozen, what, in reality, is fluid. They box, label, and categorize life. Our words then separate us from the world, from each other, from ourselves.

For example, if I get up in the morning and my mind says, "Oh, yes, another Monday," I am already boxing up this day, shutting it away from me, separating myself from it, before I have even touched or tasted it. In actuality, it is not "another Monday" at all. Even the label "Monday" is a creation of language, a box to put the day in. When we use language in this way, it shuts down the process of our seeing, our knowing, our feeling. Our words promote blindness. Our words kill our wonder and deaden the world around us. Our words keep us from entering the river of life.

Our journal work helps us let go of categories and see with our own eyes. For this day, this "Monday," has never been before and never will be again. It is unique, different from all other days since time and days began. It is precious far beyond my small knowing. It is unique to me alone, for it is my day. No one else will have the same day that I have. If we are not careful, if we do not look closely with our seeing and saying, we are as limited as the proverbial blind man who touched the elephant: We experience but a tiny part of the creature, yet in the audacity and ignorance of our small knowing, we box it up and pronounce, "This is the elephant. This is the truth. This is life."

In our journals, we use words in a different way, watching carefully and finding another way to be, another world to live in. As we work in this second way with our words, letting go of preconceived categories and labels, as we learn to wonder with our words, the world opens unto us. In this way, we learn to use our words, as the Buddhists say, as "fingers pointing at the moon"—the wondrous, ineffable moon of reality, which can never be captured or contained, which can only be pointed at.

Approaching the world and our words in this way, we find that as we say what we see (that is, as we observe and write in our journals), we come to see more. And as we see more, we have more to say; and as we say more, we see even more. And on and on, seeing and saying, saying and seeing, spiraling out of boredom and into wonder As e.e. cummings writes at the end of his prayer-poem "i thank you God for most this amazing": "(now the ears of my ears awake and / now the eyes of my eyes are opened)." And so it continues, over and over again as we do this work.

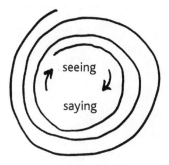

This is the human writing-learning process: We see and then we say (write), and our saying-writing leads to further seeing and further saying—our ears awakening, our eyes opening, again and again.

The key to opening yourself to this world, the way to practice wondering with your words, is to avoid making absolute statements or generalizations in your journal ("The world is evil" . . . "My husband is wrong" . . . "Mondays are terrible" . . . "My boss is a jerk"). Instead, describe how things look right now and say how you feel right now. Make all observations tentatively, speculatively, wonderingly. Ask yourself questions. Use your words delicately and gently. Stay open. Keep looking. Let go. Let go. Let go. In this way, your words will keep your eyes open instead of closing them.

In the film *On Golden Pond*, after Chelsea says her father does not love her, her mother responds: "Your father does love you—and if you don't see that it's because you haven't looked closely enough." In your journal work, practice looking closely at your words. In this way, you stay open to the world—and the world continues to open unto you. You learn to trust that, as you see things that hurt you and make you small and hold you back, you will let go of them and move naturally toward health and wholeness. You learn there are great powers within you.

EXPLORATION

Freeing the Writer Within

Like so many of your other "selves," your writing self has often been boxed up and mistreated and abused—made to feel small, inadequate, or dumb. As with your other selves, letting go of those boxes and getting to know that self better, attending to its wounds and hurts and fears, and letting it tell its stories will help free your writing self. This is especially important if you are entering the writing-and-being process for the first time. Often, your writing self has little idea what it is capable of, how much power it has. Like your other selves, it needs to be healed and encouraged and nurtured.

Be still for a while. Relax and breathe deeply. As you breathe, feel your mind letting go, just watching and being.

- **Go inside to the writer within you.** Remember the things that happened to that writer—the teachings, the wounds, the joys. As you breathe, watch that self, your writing self.

- **Write what you remember of your writer's life.** Open your journal and write down bits you can remember of the life of your writing self. Don't worry about getting the pieces in the right order or even whether the facts are correct. Just record whatever you can remember. Here are some suggestions to help nudge this remembering:

  - Write down any memories you have of writing before you went to school.

  - Recall your first school memories of writing—your teachers, what you wrote about.

- Record positive school memories of writing—what you wrote that you were praised for, what you took home and taped to the refrigerator.

- Recall negative school memories involving writing—writing as punishment, writing something you cared about and then receiving a poor grade on it.

- Explore how writing was valued and modeled in your home as you were growing up—when you saw your parents writing, when you were encouraged to write.

- Explore how you feel about your writing and yourself as a writer now.

This writing-remembering will get you started on knowing, healing, and nurturing the writer within. As you continue keeping your journal, other memories and feelings will come back to you. Continue to collect them and attend to them in your journal work.

Toward Public Writing

From your "Freeing the Writer Within" Exploration, focus on one thing—an incident, a person, a memory, a recurring theme—and explore it further. With your words, keep pushing at the edges of what you see and remember. Then work this remembrance into a form (a poem, letter, vignette, story) to share with others. You could choose the time a teacher put your picture and words on the wall in second grade; the time you had to stay in and write two hundred times, "I will not . . ."; the pen pal you never met; the time a teacher posted your intercepted love note to Billie Doyle on the bulletin board. It is all there in your memory. Let your writing self tell its stories—and share them with others.

Kathy did this Exploration in my "Methods of Teaching English" class, where we worked on how to teach writing to others in a meaningful way. Students kept journals and wrote memories of their writing selves. Here is what Kathy shared with the class:

Something Missing in My Writing—Me

The day I stopped drinking, I started writing again. That was one year, two months, six hours, and twenty-seven minutes ago. I'll never forget it. I was so drunk I couldn't get off the bathroom floor—and didn't want to. I wanted to die. Intellectually, I realized I was killing myself and those who loved me. But I seemed powerless to control the nightmare. I wanted to wake up, but I couldn't.

My mother, who has dealt with her own bottle-demons, asked me that day if I still kept a journal. I realized it had been a long time since I had written anything except academic-jargon research papers. I always got A's, but there was something missing in my writing. Me.

That day, I was too sick to go to work, too sick to get dressed, too sick to answer the phone. Because I had classes on Tuesdays and Thursdays, I always got drunk on those nights, knowing I didn't have to go to class the next day. Oh, I was wise. I was also killing myself. That day, something told me the only way out was to write. So, all day long, I sat in my house, writing. When it got so bad I could think of nothing except the booze, I wrote some more. I wrote letters to all my relatives, letters to the editors of newspapers, letters to my daughter, which I never delivered. I copied recipes, updated my Christmas card list, and cried through my poetry.

I made it through that day—and I have made it through all the succeeding days since. I started keeping a journal again. It was like a diary at first—what I did, whom I spoke to, and what happened in the world that day. Gradually, I began to realize that I drank in order to avoid my feelings. Finding them again through writing was a slow, tough process.

I not only had to find my feelings; I had to find me on paper. Why, when I proofread most of my writing, did I sound like a stranger? Who was this woman who wrote all these fancy, correct sentences and dull papers—and then went home and got drunk?

Gradually, I found myself and my own voice in my journal. Now, I am sober. Now, my writing has voice because it has me.

EXPLORATION

Word Photos

As you work on writing in your journal, you are working on both your seeing and your saying. As you write to say what you see, you will begin to understand more—so you will have more to say, which in turn will lead to more seeing. And so you will go on in this work, spiraling into awareness.

In a way, you will use your words as a photographer uses a camera—you will become more alert, see more. There is a potential picture everywhere. There is meaning in everything. You will experience your life more fully—stopping to look at and touch things you had hurried by before. Little things will begin to blossom with meaning and beauty. It is all there, waiting.

Take a few special minutes with your journal by your side just to sit and breathe and quiet yourself.

- **Go back over your day in search of small "photos."** Review your day, looking for those small moments like pictures in your mind.

- **Write in your journal the moments that come to you.** Watch for those deceptively simple "nothings" that are waiting for you to discover them: the tear-stained face of a child peering from the school bus window as you stopped at the traffic light; the two mourning doves pushed against each other on a long, empty stretch of the power line; the dead cat at the edge of rush-hour traffic; the rare childlike vulnerability on your father's face as he lay asleep in his chair after dinner.

- **As you write, do not "explain" what you see; just see it fully with your words.** Keep your words grounded in your five senses. How did it look, feel, smell, taste, sound? See it in new ways, from other perspectives, from another angle. Move around it with your words. Wait for the lighting to change.

Toward Public Writing

In our journals, we may start by using lots of words—searching, wondering, poking around, trying to see what is there. We play with images and metaphors to see what fits. We look for words that work. And then, as we get an angle on the feeling we want to record, as we get at the heart of it, we begin to work our way back toward a few strong words. We pare it down. We eliminate words that aren't precise. We tighten. We focus.

In this way, we are also working toward an effective piece of public writing, a "photo" of a meaningful moment for others to enter and learn from. In some ways, the essence of a word photo is the essence of all good public writing—to get a few carefully chosen words to point beyond themselves to greater meaning.

Recently, I wrote a poem about my visit home after an absence of two years. The poem is about what happens when the feelings are so strong, so close, you cannot write about them—so you write about not being able to write:

There are so many things
to write about, he thought,
remembering how his grandmother
lay so small on the white bed,
her legs side by side, like two sticks,
her body dwindling to bone;
remembering old Emil's eyes
gone to milky blue
and the round, pink scar
etched upon his temple;
remembering how his mother
groped with her hands
beyond the fading light
and how his father
coughed in the night—

but the pen grew heavy
in his hand,
and he went out
to count the stars instead.

This poem emerged from four simple photos I had recorded in my journal—of my grandmother in the nursing home; of old Emil, who tried to kill himself; of my mother, whose eyesight was failing; of my father, who smoked too much.

This is what you work toward—strong, lean words, words that awaken your ears and open your eyes to the world around you. Use words that help you to see, even as you craft them for others to see.

Work some of your journal photos into pieces of public writing to share with your writing group. You might want to limit yourself to seventy-five or a hundred words per photo. The key is to make every word count. Give each piece a title and arrange them on a sheet of paper, like mounted photographs. Or weave several word photos together to show something or someone larger.

EXPLORATION

So Much Depends

Years ago, as an undergraduate English major, I read William Carlos Williams' simple little poem called "The Red Wheelbarrow." The poem consists of just an image:

so much depends
upon

a red wheel
barrow

glazed with rain
water

beside the white
chickens

At the time, I remember being mystified by the poem. Having been properly trained in literary criticism, I wondered what the real meaning of the poem was, what it was really about. Now I know: It is about "a red wheelbarrow glazed with rainwater beside the white chickens." And now I know, for me, "so much depends upon" so many little images, so many little memories—and upon my ability to see them and say them.

What is left out of Williams' poem is the fact that when he conceived that image he was sitting at the bedside of a very sick child. (Williams was a medical doctor.) The story goes that as he sat there, deeply concerned about the child, he looked out the window, saw that image, and penned those words.

This Exploration involves our being aware of and collecting in our journals images from both sides of that equation.

Our days are filled with moments and images that hurt and sadden us—and with contrasting moments and images that comfort and sustain us. Here, we attend to and work with both.

- **As you carry your journal with you through the day, watch for specific small things that bother you, sadden you, anger you.** Note the person who cuts you off in traffic, the killings on the evening news, the billboards along the freeway, whatever. Watch and be aware, and write them down in your journal.

- **At the same time, watch for and collect in your journal images of little things that please you, hearten you, give you hope.** Write of the child who waves as you go by the playground, the mockingbird singing on the power-line above the alley, the crescent moon just above the horizon.

Just being aware of and articulating these things in your journal—the negative and the positive—will help you. But they can also become the heart of your own poetry, in the way of William Carlos Williams.

Toward Public Writing

Look back over the negative and positive images that you have collected in your journal. Work on combining them into your own "So much depends upon . . ." poems. Williams' poem leaves out the negative, the sick child. For our purposes, put in a negative image first—and then its contrast, a positive image. The idea is: "Because of this (negative), so much depends on this (positive)."

Work with clean, small, contrasting images to carry your message—nothing more. Write without telling; just show the images. Try to come up with four or five such small poems, each no more than forty-five words or so, and use the title to help set up your contrast.

Here, for example, are three that recently found their way out of my life and into my journal and then into these public poems:

On Highway #87
Crossing the Verde River
As the Ford F-350 with the gun rack
And the NRA sticker
Roars past me,
So much depends upon
The blue heron standing silent

In the river
Beside the willows.

At the Faculty Meeting

As the gray voices drone on
Intoning the Gods of Grants
And Deconstruction and Publication
So much depends upon
The memory of the old man's holy words
In the darkness of the sweatlodge.

To My Students

Listening to my colleague
With her stainless steel contacts
Bitch about her students, I smile:
So much depends upon
The fragments of your words
I carry in the pocket of my heart.

As we do this work, we are giving voice to and acknowledging both our grievances and our delights. By taking them out of us and giving them a form and sharing them, we simultaneously devalue the negatives in our lives and revalue the positives. Such is the magic and the power of this writing work.

You can continue to collect such images of grievances and delights as you do your daily journal work. And then, when the spirit or the occasions calls, you can move them into such public pieces—and continue to learn from them.

five

Centering in the Self

There can never be peace between nations until there is first known that true peace which is within the souls of men. This comes when men realize their oneness with the universe and all its Powers, and when they know that the Great Spirit is at its center . . . and that this center is really everywhere, it is within each of us.

—BLACK ELK

Asking the Questions

Fundamental to the transformational power of journal writing is an inevitable movement toward a Center within ourselves—a Center that is love and that changes everything. This love is not the small "commodity love" we have been taught. This is not love to earn points for heaven. This is a love that requires no rule book, no "shoulds" and "should nots," no worry about right and wrong. This is love as natural as breathing. This is a love that feels like coming home.

It has taken me a long time to see this in my life. Growing up in an alcoholic family, for example, I was taught that love and anger were mutually incompatible, that I could not love someone and be angry at them simultaneously. I learned, therefore, to suppress my anger, to hide it, to deny it even from myself. That part of me, the self that was angry, was denied, and my anger was repressed and stored—until eventually some small incident would burst the dam, and the anger would spew forth. When this happened, it frightened me because I saw that my anger had taken control, that I had no choices. In those frightening moments, I saw that I did not have anger, I was my anger; I did not like that feeling. It was then, following some whispering intuition, that I began to keep a journal, and things began to change for me.

As we write in our journals, we are, in effect, talking to ourselves. Invariably, one of the fundamental questions we are working on, then, whether or not we are aware of it, is: "Who am I?" It is a question we are seldom encouraged to ask, for it brings with it other questions, such as: "Why am I here?," "What is my purpose in life?," and "What matters?"

We are not often encouraged to ask such questions because they inevitably lead us inside ourselves for the answers. Such questions do not make us good consumers or good followers. From childhood, we have been taught by the media and advertising and even our schooling that what we seek is outside ourselves. We have been told that the answers are out there somewhere—and that they are for sale, if we can make enough money, or for the taking, if we can get enough power.

Watching Our Many Selves

Though we may not even be aware of it, much of our journal writing is a process of watching those "I"s, those small selves that are a part of us, but not all of us. In this way, our journal writing allows us to gain perspective on our lives; it allows us to be more aware of our actions and feelings, even as we are doing them and feeling them. To take the example of my anger: When I write my anger in my journal, I am actually watching the "I" that is angry. Or, when I write about my hurt from my childhood, I am watching the "I" that is that child within me, still hurting. When I write about my fear, I am watching the "I" that is afraid.

The key to the transformational power of this writing process, then, is something like this: As I write about my anger, I am watching my anger. If I am watching my anger, then the anger is only one part of me, not all of me. I am not trapped in it. I am not my anger. I may have anger, but I am not my anger. There is a great and crucial difference between having anger and being anger. When I am my anger, when it consumes me, when I cannot watch it, cannot watch the "I" that is angry, then that "I," or that angry self, is in control. Then the rest of me has no choices but the angry self's choices. I am at its mercy. Then I cannot act; I can only react.

The great power of journal writing is that it enables us, without our having to know or understand consciously how it works, to begin living our lives actively rather than reactively. As we work in our journals, we make choices we could not make before, because we could not see, because we were trapped in the small vision of that partial identity. We live more creatively and begin to become the artists of our own lives.

I frequently see dramatic examples of this freeing power of writing. A few summers ago, for example, I taught a writing class for Hispanic high school students. These students were bused to the university campus from the barrios of south Phoenix. Many of them were poor; for most of them, violence was a daily part of their lives. Doreen was a student in that class. She was seventeen and would be a senior in the fall. In the course of our five weeks together, it became obvious from things she said and wrote that she was in an abusive and potentially violent relationship with a man. In a poem she titled "Fear," she wrote:

> Fear is seeing girls
> beaten to death on the news
> and knowing you're not too far from that.
> Fear is seeing someone who loves you
> hitting you over and over
> and not knowing when it's going to stop.
> Fear is seeing yourself
> forgiving all the pain
> and being too weak to stop it. . . .

During our time together, I said nothing directly to Doreen about this issue, nor did she to me. But about three weeks after the class ended, I received a letter from her that contained the following:

> You showed me a whole new, endless world of writing, inside something very important—me. Writing feelings down and turning them into something to share has allowed me to see inside myself. You have reminded me of something I seem to have forgotten. That I am important. Because of you, I have just left a relationship that was both mentally and physically abusive. After three and a half years, leaving was the hardest thing to do, but I did it. . . . I know I deserved better than what I had, because nobody deserves that. . . . I'll get through it.

Although Doreen says, "You showed me . . ." and "You have reminded me . . ." and "Because of you . . . ," I actually had very little to do with what she discovered. She did this herself, through her writing. The movement from Doreen's small self, the one trapped in that relationship, toward her Center, toward her Self, allowed her to see and to choose and to save herself.

Moving to the Center

All of this points to a crucial question: If, when I write in my journal, I am watching myself—who is the "I" that is watching?

Just as a camera cannot take a picture of itself, my anger, for example, cannot watch itself. So, when I am writing my anger, I am in some small way moving to a place beyond my anger. In the section above, we learned that when Doreen wrote about her fear (and this happens with all of us), she began moving to a place that watches, a place beyond her fear. What is that place? Who is the "I" that watches the "I"? I do not know—nor does anyone else.

Since whatever is going on when this transcendence happens lies far beyond the understanding of the left brain; it can only be described in metaphor. Think of it this way: We have many small selves that are the parts we play, the many people that we are. But beyond these small selves is the Self, the "I" that lies beyond the "I"s, beyond the roles, beyond our ego, beyond our small seeing. Envision it as something like this:

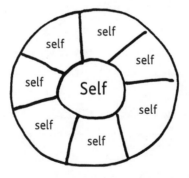

When I am writing in my journal, I am usually not even aware that this watching process is happening but the act of writing nevertheless moves me out of the small self I am writing about and into the "I" that watches, the "I" that is my Center, my greater Self. This Center Self lies beyond the struggles of our small selves. It is the Self that has been denied us because it does not exist within a left-brained, materialistic picture of the world. It is, if you will, a place of peace that passes understanding, a place of love, a place beyond the ego, the competition, the judging of the left brain.

Nearly everything in modern society pushes us outward into our small selves, telling us that these outer selves are who we are. And of course, we must play these parts; we are these parts we play. But the questions, then, follow: How do I play them?" and who am I when I lose them?

When we begin to look at the Self, an ironic truth emerges: The more I am centered in my Self, the healthier I am and the better I do in my smaller selves. And conversely: The more I cling to my smaller selves as my identity, the less effective and healthy I am in those identities. For example, the more I am caught up in my identity as professor, and the more my ego needs that identity, the less effective, healthy, creative, and free I am in that identity. If my primary sense of self is in my identity as "Dr. Nelson," then I will always be protecting that identity. I will always be on the defensive—watching for attacks upon this "me," worried about making a fool of myself, looking for ways to get promoted in order to enhance myself. I will get involved in playing politics and saving face and one-upmanship. I will have little energy or attention left to care about my students, to see what their needs are, to be creative in my teaching.

The same rule applies to all my identities, all my smaller selves. The more I am centered in my Self, the better I will be as parent and husband, the better I will be able to deal with my fear and my anger, and so on. Focusing on the Self does not mean that I cease to care about the other parts of me, these identities I have. Indeed, I am freed to care more because, coming from my Center, I am not trapped in the part; I am not at the mercy of that identity. I can play the part better because my action comes from my Center Self through that identity. I can dance with it.

One good test for checking my centeredness is this: Can I laugh at myself? For if I can laugh at a particular self, I can step back from it. I am not trapped in it. My ego is not greatly involved in it. In the midst of teaching, for example, can I stop and laugh at a mistake I have made? If I can, then I am a healthier teacher. If I can laugh, then it is really no mistake at all, and I have a wonderful freedom. And I have modeled an important lesson for my students. It does not mean that I value my "self" less as a teacher but that I value my Self more.

What about you? Can you smile at yourself as a parent dealing with your children? Can you smile at the "you" that thinks you are dying because your lover has left you? Can you laugh at yourself as a feminist? Or a man? Or an environmentalist? Or a vegetarian? Or a Republican? Check it out.

Another test is: Who am I if I lose that self? If, for example, much of my identity is wrapped up in being "Professor Nelson," and if I come to work tomorrow and find a letter saying that my services are no longer needed at the university, who am I then? Do I have a Center? Can I survive? Was that identity all of me? Or suppose I go home tonight and find a note on the door from my wife saying my services are no longer needed? Who am I then? Or who am I as my children grow up and leave to have lives of their own and my identity as a parent diminishes? Or who am I if my house burns down and I lose all my possessions?

In doing this writing-and-being work, I have begun to see what Jesus meant when he suggested it might be harder for a rich man to find heaven than for a camel to pass through the eye of a needle. It is so easy for my riches, my "things," my identities, to pull me away from my Center, my Self. And then I smile, remembering the old Buddhist who wrote in his journal something to this effect: "Since my house burned down, I now have a much better view of the full moon rising." Who is free? Who is truly rich?

We do this watching work, this journal work, so that we might be centered in our greater Self, so that we might find peace and love within ourselves—and give peace and love to others.

EXPLORATION

Who Am I?

Once you get hold of the idea that every "I" is a "we," that you are made up of many small selves, the power of your personal writing will become more understandable and more available to you. It works something like this: The more you write, the more you become aware of your small selves; the more you become aware of your small selves, the more you become centered in the greater Self. This Exploration will help promote awareness of your small selves.

Find a quiet place. Settle your body. Quiet your mind by attending to your breathing for a few minutes.

- **Review your day, watching for all the different roles you played.** Look for all the different selves you were during just this one day. Look at when you were "friend," when you were "parent," when you were your job identity, etc. Observe the different feelings that came with those different identities.

- **In your journal, list the major roles you play in your life.** List each role carefully and deliberately, in this way: "I am _____." Fill in each identity and self that comes to mind. Consider such identities as:

  General identities:

  I am my physical body.
  I am my emotions.
  I am my intellect.
  I am a male (or female).

Relationship identities:

I am the son of my father.
I am a husband.
I am a friend (of John, of Edith, etc.)
I am a sister.

Job and "doing" identities:

I am a teacher.
I am a student.
I am a writer.
I am a runner.

Belonging identities:

I am a Democrat.
I am a feminist.
I am a Rotarian.

Religious identities:

I am a Buddhist.
I am a Methodist.
I am an agnostic.

Ethnic identities:

I am Native American.
I am Anglo.
I am Asian.

Possession identities:

I am my house.
I am my Porsche.
I am my clothes.

By now, you probably have a list of at least twenty or so of your own most prominent selves and identities. Keep this list in your journal, and add to it as you become aware of other identities, other parts you play.

The act of writing in your journal leads to fundamental changes in your life because it shows you that you are made up of many "I"s, that you play many parts and have many selves. You will also develop a sense of a greater Self that lies beyond these smaller selves. Once you see that, you are seeing the frame around the picture: You are no longer trapped in those "I"s, those small selves.

Toward Public Writing

Go over the identities you have listed in your journal. Focus on one of your selves, one that is struggling in some way. Perhaps your "child self" is struggling in your relationship with a parent, or your "job self" is unhappy in the work you are doing, or your "student self" is struggling in school.

Focusing on the self that you have chosen, write a description in third person of that self and what it is struggling with and how it is feeling. Write about some of that self's options to improve, change, or heal the situation. Say, for example, I choose to write about my job self, which is feeling trapped, stagnant, and unchallenged. My description might go something like this:

These feelings of boredom and stagnation have been slowly growing in him for a long time. Only recently has he noticed how strong they have grown—and he wonders if this is also why he has been feeling depressed a lot in the last year. . . . He sees no way to change the situation—except to quit. He hasn't really faced that option. I think it is too scary for him right now. Still, he could talk to his family about it and hear what they say.

You get the idea. See what happens for you. Give the piece a title and share it with others. It will help them and you.

EXPLORATION

Talking to Your Selves

As you do this watching work in your journal, you will become able to watch your small selves even in the moment, even when those selves are doing things. One day, for example, I was on the phone with a friend and fellow writer whom I had asked to read and give me feedback on the manuscript for this book. At one point, she told me that my Explorations were too long and wordy. As she talked, I watched my writer self feeling hurt and wanting to pout. If I had been trapped in that self, not able to watch it, I would probably have reacted in anger or self-pity. Instead, I laughed gently with my writer self and listened to my friend and learned a thing or two. My Center Self had choices that my writer self did not have.

Sit quietly with your journal by your side and breathe deeply for awhile. And then:

- **In your journal, practice writing dialogues between particular small selves and your Center Self.** For example, write a dialogue between one of your selves that is struggling in some way and your Center Self. Write as though they were talking to each other. Let your small self start the conversation by telling your Center Self what the problem is, and then let them talk freely. Write it in script form, like this:

TEACHER SELF: I wanted to talk to you because lately I have been feeling very discouraged. I just don't feel satisfied or believe that I am doing a good job with the kids anymore.

CENTER SELF: I'm glad you came to talk to me. I am always here for you, whether you know it or not. Tell me more about your teaching. You have always been excited about teaching. When did it start to change?

As you switch back and forth, writing the dialogue for each self (and Self), let your consciousness move from one to the other. Let each speak as freely and genuinely as possible. As you get comfortable with this format, you will be amazed at what your various small selves can gain from talking to your Center Self.

Toward Public Writing

Pick a dialogue from your journal, and work it into a short scene between two characters. Give it the feel of an actual play script. Embody your small self in one of the characters and your Center Self in the other. Put them in a setting, and give them names; let them talk to each other, and see what happens. Give the scene some sort of natural beginning, let the dialogue run its course, and then let it conclude in some natural way.

Here, for example, is an excerpt from a dialogue by a man in one of my workshops. He called it "Except as You Become a Child":

CHILD SELF: Sometimes I wish we had not even started this journal writing stuff. Maybe it was better when I was just hiding, when I was not even acknowledged. When I did not even have a voice. Now I feel such pain sometimes—and these stories just keep coming out.

CENTER SELF: But were you happy then? Hadn't you numbed yourself so you could hide? I know this is painful for you—but don't you also feel more alive than you did before?

CHILD SELF: That's easy for you to say . . . but I guess it is true—except sometimes when it all comes pouring out of me and seems too much to bear. That last story I wrote, about my father beating my mother and I couldn't do anything about it . . . in the middle of writing that, I started to cry. I cried harder and more deeply than I have cried since I was—well, since I was a child.

CENTER SELF: I know. I was right there with you. Did you forget?

CHILD SELF: I suppose so. This is all so new, being aware that you are here with me, that I don't have to carry it all, that I can tell you about it and let go of it. That I can cry. And maybe one day sing and dance again.

As the student read this piece to the class, he cried. We could feel the healing taking place. We could hear it in his voice; we could see it in his face. In his sharing, he gave us a great gift. Do this work for yourself and experience its power.

EXPLORATION

Writing How-To Instructions

A couple of years ago, I received a birth announcement from a friend. On the front of the announcement was a heading that read, "How to Really Love a Child." Under that heading was a long listing of specific ways to love a child, things like: "Hug trees with your child," "bake a cake together and eat it with your hands," "go find elephants and kiss them," "mail letters to God," "plant licorice in your garden," "let them bang on pots and pans." It went on in this manner, listing about twenty such specific ways to love your child.

The piece was effective and fun because it grounded the instructions in simple, specific, imaginative ways to love a child. I liked the concept, and so (as is my way as a writing teacher) I stole it and turned it into an Exploration. I then tried it out on one of my classes and got back some delightfully imaginative and creative responses. Try it yourself and see what happens.

Open your journal and sit quietly for a few moments.

- **Think about things and issues in your life that might be fun and instructive to turn into a how-to listing.** Write these possibilities down in your journal. List topics that have personal meaning for you, that come from your heart, from your struggles, your life (e.g., "How to Love Your Parents" or "How to Study for a Test" or "How to Survive When Your Lover Leaves You" or "How to Survive When Your Lover Won't Leave You.")

- **Pick one, for now, that calls out to you.** List that one at the top of a blank page in your journal—and then, for ten or fifteen minutes, just write down all kinds of specific how-to's that come to your mind in relation to that topic. Be imaginative and creative. Have fun with it. Learn from it.

Toward Public Writing

Now, pick out twelve or fifteen or so of the best ones from your journal listing, and begin weaving them into a public piece. Pick some funny ones, some serious ones, some crazy ones.

The form for this public piece is quite simple. Your title is your how-to topic—and the piece consists solely of your listing. For simplicity and consistency, make the listing in the form of imperative sentences. (What? You've forgotten? They are sentences with the subject implied. They direct *you* to do something—as in, "Clean your room," "Wash your hands," or "Bring me my mint julep." Got it?)

To help you get a feel for this, here is one written by Jason, one of my Navajo students:

How to Herd Sheep

Wake up before the sun rises. Wash with icy cold water. Eat yesterday's fry bread and potatoes. Greet the sheep dogs. Let the sheep out of the corral and follow them. Draw pictures in the sand. Sit on a rock and sing to the sheep. Fall asleep under a cedar tree. Check on the sheep. Tell the dogs what you learned in school. Run to the top of the hill. Run down the other side and jump the rock. Climb the windmill. Take a swim in the water tank. Ride the ram. Herd the sheep back to the corral. Take roll call. Go home to a hot bowl of mutton stew and fry bread. It's a hard job, but someone has to do it.

As you can see, Jason had fun with this. But as he read it in the Feather Circle, that sacred place where we pass the story-stick and share our writing, he was smiling nostalgically. As we listened, we could tell that it brought back sweet memories for him, memories of home, and we smiled along with him.

And here is one that I wrote at a time when I was struggling with the politics and values of the institution where I work:

How to Teach at ASU and Still Stay Alive

Don't take yourself so damn seriously. Allow no one to use obscene words like "pedagogy," "heuristic," and "rubric" in your presence. Call 911 and report that you have been abducted and are being held against your will in a UFO (University Faculty Office). Vow to go to no more than one meeting a week. If that meeting is boring (is the Pope Catholic?), take off your clothes and stand on your chair. At least once an hour, glance out your little hermetically sealed, slit-window so you don't forget the sky. Burn some sage and sweet-grass and pray every morning (and invite the campus police to join you when they come by to check for "controlled substances"). Do at least as much me-search as research. Enroll in your own classes. Listen carefully to your students. Look into their eyes. Be sure your syllabus includes laughter and tears. Invite the Native American students to hold the spring powwow in your office. Always keep that satellite photo of the wondrous blue marble of the Earth on your wall to remind you of your real office.

I felt better when I finished writing that—and better still when I read it in the Feather Circle with my class. Try it with one item from your list. And then another. As always, if you do it carefully, you will feel your words teaching you and helping you, even as you write.

six

Exploring the Kingdom Within

For the brain, though the size of a grapefruit, is as vast as the universe.

— JUDITH HOOPER AND DICK TERESI,
THE THREE-POUND UNIVERSE

The Amazing Gift

Nobody tells us about our brain. It just sits there—about the size of a grapefruit—at the top of our spinal column. It weighs only about three pounds. Nobody tells us it is the most complex piece of matter yet found in the universe. Nobody tells us that it is a miracle, that we are miracles.

Nobody tells us that there was no reason—no logical, linear, scientific, mechanistic, Darwinistic, survival-of-the-species reason—for the human neocortex to emerge sometime between 100,000 and 40,000 years ago. And along with it, and somehow intricately a part of it, came language—the ability to utter sounds and create marks with which we might convey meaning to one another.

No one tells us that this whole neocortex-language thing is apparently some mysterious gift—*from* we know not where, *for* we know not what. But most certainly, we were meant to use this amazing gift for more than the mere memorization of facts or the reiteration of information, things we so often do in the name of education. And most certainly, this brain can give us more of life than we are taught to seek in the American dream.

Yet there it sits, at the top of our spinal column—the human brain. Scientists tell us the brain works something like a computer, as if that were some immense concession to its ability. But they do not tell us that, compared to the human brain, the most complex computer yet constructed is but a Tinkertoy set. They do not tell us that our brain—yours and mine, the average human neocortex—has from 50 billion to 100 billion cells and that each of those cells has from 5,000 to 50 thousand connections with the cells around it. This gives the brain something like 100 trillion synapses (which are, in the computer metaphor, "bytes"). They do not tell us that a computer with that kind of capacity, even given the latest technology, would have to be huge—and even if we could somehow build it, it could not yet do all the amazing things our brains can do.

Yet there it sits, at the top of our spinal column, weighing just three pounds. And nobody points out that the probability that this amazing human brain would evolve randomly from the chemical ooze of primeval oceans to what it is today—the probability of this happening merely by chance (which is how we have been told it happened)—is about the same as the probability of a tornado blowing through a junkyard and randomly assembling a fully functioning Boeing 747 jumbo jet.

Nobody asks us to wonder how this might have happened, what might be possible, where we might be heading, what we might be becoming. Nobody suggests that the human brain is a miracle, that we are miracles. Nobody tells us that we might dream greater dreams than the little plastic and tinsel we have been offered. Nobody acts amazed. Mostly, we just blunder on—bored miracles.

Different Realities

We enter our journals, our writing and being, looking for greater things. As background for this work, it helps to understand the implications of some insights we have gained over the years into the amazing workings of the human brain. Over the last twenty or thirty years, researchers have discovered some revolutionary insights about the brain, especially about its bimodal nature. At the least, these insights should be revolutionary. Actually, though, most of us have not changed much in response to this new information. But the potential is still there, waiting for us to see it, claim it.

To begin with, scientists have discovered that the human cerebral cortex is divided into two halves or hemispheres—the right brain and the left brain—and that these two halves tend to function in different ways. In some ways, they are two separate "brains"; they perceive, know, and understand in different ways. They are in touch with different realities, different worlds, different ways of being.

From what we can tell so far, our left brain perceives, knows, and understands things logically, linearly, rationally, and analytically. Our left brain sees things as happening in a line, sequentially, with one thing leading logically to the next—cause and effect, stimulus and response, Simon and Garfunkel. The left brain understands things by taking them apart, analyzing them, dissecting them. It does not see patterns well. It sees the parts, the trees, but has trouble seeing the whole, the forest.

Our right brain perceives, knows, and understands more intuitively, metaphorically, imaginatively, and holistically. Our right brain sees patterns, wholes, gestalts. It sees relationships—how things come together, how things are alike. It dreams and imagines and feels. If our left brain sees the trees, our right brain sees the forest. If our left brain is smart and enterprising, our right brain is wise and loving.

Remembering that the right side of the brain controls the left side of the body (and vice versa), we might say that the symbol of the left-brained approach to life and learning is the right fist. It seeks to understand by organizing and controlling. The right brain is symbolized by the open left hand. Its approach to life and learning is receptive. It seeks no gain. It does not see the world in terms of either-or, right-wrong, win-lose. The right brain has soft eyes. It is our beginner's mind.

Much of what we know thus far about the nature of the right and left halves of our brain we have learned from the experiences of people who have had "split-brain" operations. As a treatment for severe epilepsy, physicians developed a technique for surgically severing the corpus callosum (the bundle of nerves and fibers connecting the two hemispheres of the cerebral cortex). Neurosurgeons initially speculated that this procedure would isolate the grand mal seizures to one side of the brain and thereby greatly reduce their severity. The neurosurgeons were correct. The surgery worked. But the next question was: What are the side effects of such a radical treatment?

Surprisingly, there are almost no outward and overt side effects from surgically severing the two sides of the brain. The procedure is not debilitating, and those who have had it tend to function quite normally thereafter. This is all the more fascinating because the corpus callosum is a large bundle of nerves and fibers that has apparently evolved to carry messages between the two sides of the brain. Exactly why split-brain surgery has no side effects is an interesting subject for speculation.

Inner Knowing

For a long time, it has been general knowledge that the right side of the brain controls the left side of the body and the left side of the brain controls the right side of the body. With that in mind, consider what right-left brain researchers have recently learned about language and the human brain.

First, research with split-brain patients has established that the ability to use language—to speak, read, and write—is usually located in the left brain. Our left brain has language. Remembering that, consider further two typical experiments done with split-brain patients that reveal interesting insights into the relationship between language and human knowing.

In one experiment, researchers had a split-brain patient put his hands behind his back (so he could not "cheat" by using his eyes to pass the information from one side of the brain to the other). The researchers then placed an object in the patient's hand and asked him to feel the object and tell them what it was. For example, they would put a ball in his right hand (which feeds into his left brain, which has language) and ask what it was. He would feel the object and say, "I have a ball in my hand." He could always verbally identify objects placed in his right hand.

However, when they placed objects in his left hand (which feeds into his right brain, which does not have language), he could not identify them. When they placed a pencil, for example, in his left hand and asked him what it was, he could not tell them. But then, to further test what his right brain knew, the researchers put several different objects in front of the patient under a cloth (again, so he could not cross the information over with his eyes). They asked him to feel among the objects with his left hand and see if he could find what he had just held in his hand (and been unable to name). The subject felt the many objects, retrieved the pencil, and held it up before the researchers.

This leaves us with a fascinating question: Did this man "know" he had a pencil in his hand or didn't he? In a larger sense, the real question is: What does it mean to "know"?

In a similar experiment, researchers devised a machine whereby they could show separate pictures to each side of a subject's brain. Working with a woman who had had a split-brain operation, they hooked her up to the machine and attached biofeedback sensors to her body so they could measure her emotional responses. They began the experiment by showing the same picture to both sides of her brain. They showed a picture of a flower, for example, to both sides of her brain and asked her what she saw. "I see a flower," the woman said, and the biofeedback equipment hummed along smoothly. They showed a picture of a car to both sides of her brain. "What do you see?" "I see a car." *Hummm. Hummm.*

For a while, they continued to show identical pictures to both sides of the woman's brain. But then the researchers played a trick on her. They showed a picture of a tree to the woman's left brain (the side that has language ability) and simultaneously showed a picture of a naked man to her right brain. "What do you see?" they asked her. "I see a tree," the woman responded. But meanwhile, the biofeedback equipment was going crazy.

So the questions become: Did the woman really see more than a tree but not "know" it? And again the larger question: What does it mean to "know"?

So first we have the man who could not answer the researchers' question. He "failed" their test. Yet he ultimately held the pencil up before them. And here we have the woman who could verbally answer only, "I see a tree." Yet her bodily knowing cried out on the biofeedback machine, "I see more than a tree!"

We are left with a question we seldom ask, because to ask it is revolutionary, to ask it is to mess with the frame of the window through which we see, the paradigm we have been given. We are left with the question: *What does it mean to "know"?*

The greatest insight of modern brain research and experiments like those described here is: *We know more than we know we know.* The corollary to that finding has generally been ignored and denied in American education—that it is, therefore, perfectly viable pedagogy to learn from ourselves. It is educational to go within, to be still, to meditate, and to talk to ourselves in our journals, in personal writing, in order to find out what we know but do not know we know.

This is why, when we work in our journals, we are not trying to write answers. This is why we write freely, openly, speculatively, wonderingly. We write to let the greater knowing, which lies within us beneath our little knowing, rise to the surface through our words. We write to find the greater Self beyond our little selves.

EXPLORATION

Maps and Memories

In this Exploration, you will draw a map. You can draw a draft of it in your journal initially, but before long it will probably take on a life of its own and want to be placed on something bigger—a large piece of newsprint or posterboard. Just as you do when you work from personal to public writing, let your map unfold in stages.

Close your eyes and breathe deeply for a while, with your journal open beside you, letting go of your immediate daily concerns.

• **Go back in your memory to when you were about ten years old.** Go gently back to the places where you lived and played, and begin to look around. Start remembering who was there and what it was like. Start remembering that child who lived there, that child who still lives within you.

- **In your journal, sketch a map of your neighborhood.** Do not be concerned about whether the map is accurate or not. Let it be a map of the world as you remember it—the streets, the trees, the houses, your house, the places you played. Some things will be bigger or smaller; some things you will remember and others you will forget to include, depending upon how they affected you and what calls out to you now. That is all right; this is your ten-year-old's map.

- **Make notes on your map to help capture your memories.** As you draw your map, memories will come pouring back. Make small annotations on your map to help you hold onto the memories, like this:

  - *My brother and I built a tree house in this old cottonwood tree.*

  - *We raced our bikes down this hill on summer nights.*

  - *Jerry lived here; he was my best friend. Nine years later, he was killed in Vietnam.*

  And on and on. Your map will blossom with memories like these, many of them wanting to turn into stories, your stories. As you work on your map, let your annotations spill over onto other pages of your journal, where they will have room to grow. Some of these stories will make you cry; some will bring a smile. But go back to them in the safety of your journal, and tell them as carefully and honestly as you can. If you cannot remember the exact details, do not worry—dream the stories, imagine them. But let them out. Your stories need to be told if you are to heal your wounds and claim your personal history and value your life. To write the stories of your past is to change your life in the present.

Toward Public Writing

You want to be a writer. You want to write poetry, short stories, novels. But where will you find all those adventures, all those characters, all those things to write about? Like the kingdom of heaven, they are not out there somewhere. They are at hand, within you. Human drama is there in the stories of your life, in your backyard when you were ten years old.

Map-memory work is the stuff of public writing, of literature. I sometimes tell my students that I assigned the "Maps and Memories" Exploration to Harper Lee and she wrote *To Kill A Mockingbird.* I say it jokingly, but that is where her novel came from—her own neighborhood when she was ten years old. She names her ten-year-old self Scout Finch and tells about the people who lived in her neighborhood and the things that happened there: her brother Jem and Mrs. Dubose down the street and Boo Radley next door, the day the rabid dog came down the street and the time they tried to steal the watermelons and on and on—history, her stories.

You can do the same. Just work the things from your map into your journal and from there into pieces of public writing. Any of your map-memories, explored and developed carefully in your journal, can be worked into meaningful stories, vignettes, and poetry for others.

Annette made her map, wrote in her journal, and remembered, and this story emerged for her:

Aunt Claire

Curtains waving from the windows said hello to the morning. I climbed onto the gossip fence and waved back. Today was Balloon

Day. The Gyder boys were inflating their homemade balloon with gas from their barbecue and preparing Leo the hamster for his solo test flight.

Red-and-white striped, the balloon was impressive. Walkie-talkies mounted on our bicycles would help us keep track of the craft. We plopped Leo into the cage and Chris shouted, "Lift off!" I sat there and watched it float up into the endless blue sky.

Wonder if Aunt Claire could see it? Aunt Claire with her too-tight dresses, which we all said looked nice. She always wore a big floppy hat over the rat's nest on her head. Mom said it was because of some kind of treatments that made her hair fall out—but I thought I could see rat tails sticking out. She used to be lots of fun, but then she just started resting and going to the doctor all the time. One day we piled into the car; I had to sit next to Aunt Claire. Her fat sat on my lap. We went to the hospital, and Mom and Aunt Claire went in. Mom came out later and we went to the park. She started crying and told us Aunt Claire was too tired to live here anymore.

The balloon was coming down fast. I hopped off the fence and waved to Aunt Claire . . . up there where only balloons can go.

Such writing, because it comes from the heart, is simple but strong and effective. If Annette had manufactured such a story (for a grade, to impress a teacher), the result could easily have been pretentious and melodramatic. But she stays with the emotional truth of the story, the feelings of a ten-year-old. The story emerges in her own language, understated and powerful. Consciously, Annette knew little about the elements of effective public writing. But we all know more than we know we know. Such abilities to see and say naturally exist in you and in your language, and they emerge when you are free to write what is real for you, when you write from your heart, and when you write without fear. Do it. You will see.

EXPLORATION

Where Are You From?

In this Exploration, we are exploring our past (which is always present within us), looking at our childhoods, our beginnings, our roots. We are working at telling our stories, which we must do in order to survive them, learn from them, grow beyond them.

Begin by opening your journal and getting quiet and receptive.

- **Consider this common question: Where are you from?** It is a question we are often asked, and we usually answer with a word or two—Omaha, Cleveland, New York. But your challenge here is to answer it with a series of images, pictures, memories.

- **Write for twenty minutes or so, just making a list of sentences.** "I am from _____." "I am from _____." "I am from _____." Complete each sentence with an image or memory or moment from your life. Explore the question fully and freely. Answer the question with images of place, of the land, of neighborhood. Answer the question with images of family, of history, of ancestry, of conception. Write and write—and discover.

To explore this question is to explore many things—your beginnings, your training, your connections, your joys and struggles, the mystery and wonder of your life.

Toward Public Writing

Now, refine these sentences—make them strong and true and grounded in the stuff of your life. And begin weaving them together in the form of a poem, a poem that doesn't rhyme but the lines sing and flow and are filled with bits and pieces of you. You can weave together images from all facets of your life; or you can focus just on images of place or images of family or images of struggle. Play with this—write and rewrite—and see what it wants to become. Give it a title. And then do another. This Exploration can easily lead to many pieces, many stories, many discoveries.

Just last week in my class I gave this Exploration. And again, I was amazed at the words that came back to me from my students, from the lives of my students. Here, for example, is Steve's piece:

Origin

Once or twice,
Probably hundreds of times,
Someone has asked me, "Where are you from?"
And I tell them Surprise, Arizona, and Evansville, Wisconsin.

What they cannot know, unless I tell them, is that I am from
*   Denmark, via my dad*
And Germany or France—or mostly the Vatican, via my mom;
That I am birthed of Allen's Creek, just as surely as I rose from it in
*   my childhood,*
Dripping as I wiped muddy bare feet on grass banks.

And surely I am of the dust on my brother's books,
the same dust that smudged my fingers

as I passed them up and down spines
dreaming of dinosaurs and Camelot.

And I am from my grandma's wagging finger
And my mother's slender stalks of rhubarb, hacked from the
    garden and fashioned into pies.

Mostly, they will think I'm giving too much information
If I tell them that I might be the result of a springtime rendezvous
In a company truck parked in a deserted cornfield,
A chance taken by two messy lives making a fresh start
In the planting season.

I'm from the past near and distant,
From a mysterious, ancient holy tradition,
Rich with prayer and incense,
That introduced me both to Jesus
And to Father Bob (who carried a beer in one hand a baseball
    mitt in the other).

I'm from dust
And little bits of God
And blood
And tears
And dreams (my own and others)
Carried on and on and on.

This is no generic, Hallmark-card piece. The power of Steve's poem comes from the careful, surprising detail, from the unique bits and pieces of his life.

And here is one that Michelle did, shorter and focusing mostly on place, but equally strong:

Beginnings

I come from the Golden State,
With waters lapping
At sun-scorched beaches
While children run and scream and build sand castles.

I come from parents who didn't get along,
Which left a wake
That still tosses me into walls
And leaves me crying in corners.

I come from two sisters,
Who aren't really mine,
But who have taught me to love and care
More than could any Hallmark card.

I come from suburbia,
With HOA mandates and manicured lawns
That I loved to roll on
Before the lawnmowers came in the morning.

Now, I come from pink sunsets,
Which face slowly over South Mountain
And leave a handful of
Pale stars against a cold sky.

Like so much of this writing-and-being work, the simple question "Where are you from?" blossoms for us into poetry and meaning. This work can lead to many insights and much public writing for you. Continue to pursue it and learn from it as you lead your writing life.

Autobiographical Poem

Before you do this Exploration, you need to do the map-memory work in the "Maps and Memories" Exploration. The map will give you the content for this Exploration.

First, just a note about poetry. These directions ask you specifically to write a poem. Do not worry about what a poem is or whether you can write one. No one knows exactly what a poem is, anyway. Think of a poem as just a shape of words on a page—whatever shape you want—a shape of words trying to see and feel life more clearly. Poetry is not restrictive. It gives your writing and being more freedom to explore. Follow the instructions and see what happens.

Begin by taking some time to quiet yourself and just breathe.

- **Reflect on your annotated map.** Gaze at it quietly for several minutes, immersing yourself again in the memories of that time.

- **Close your eyes and go back to your childhood.** Let your mind follow the flow of your life back from the present to that ten-year-old time, through that time, and back to your earliest memories. Watch for specific moments and memories that stand out for you.

- **For ten minutes, write your memories without stopping.** In stream-of-consciousness style, with no concern for the mechanics of writing, record as they come to you specific memories of all kinds from the flow of your life. Make no attempt to remember in chronological order. Make no distinction between trivial and monumental. Just record specific moments from your life for ten minutes without stopping. If it helps or feels comfortable to do so, string them together with "I remember . . . I remember . . . I remember . . ."

- **Read back over what you have written.** This reflecting-writing process will feed on itself, and the memories will keep unfolding.

- **Write more in your journal.** Expand on some of the memories that came to you, and add more that are triggered by your reading.

This kind of timed, nonstop writing is a good technique to use in your journal work any time and in relation to any topic. It will help you get beyond your left-brained knowing. It will help break down concern for the form of your writing, which sometimes gets in the way of discovery.

Toward Public Writing

For this piece of public writing, you will simply read over your timed writing and your other map-memories and share a collection of random images—little bits and pieces from your life. As you look back on your life in your journal, thousands of memories will surface in your mind. For this autobiographical poem, take a handful of these memories and sprinkle them throughout.

The stock of most poetry is imagery—word pictures. Think of this writing as some small word photos from your life. Here are some suggestions to help you get started:

- Begin with an image from your birth; make it up or fantasize it from what you imagine was going on.

- End with an image from your present life.

- In between, include many random moments, memories, images, and other word photos from your life.

- Share pictures made only of sensory things. Avoid abstractions.

From this beginning, my students have produced many powerful poems that have found their own angle of vision. As your poem starts to take off, let it become what it needs to become.

Dan, for example, was only eleven years old when he came to a journal workshop with his mother. After the mapping exercise, I gave the group some suggestions similar to those above and then gave them ten minutes to write an autobiographical poem. When the time was up, I asked if anyone would be willing to share what they had written. Dan was the first to raise his hand, and he read the following:

Dan's Autobiography

I remember the cold rain
*   beating about on the window*
*   when I was born.*
I remember when I fell asleep in my spinach.
I remember when my mom finally caught me
*   after about ten minutes of hiding*
*   and gave me a bath.*
I remember when I was two
*   and skied into a hill of snow.*

I remember jumping into a bucket of rainwater
    when I was four.
I remember when I almost drowned
    and my brother saved me.
I remember when the tractor
    came down the road
    and filled in my pothole where I kept
    everything from BBs to old scabs
    that I tore off my arm.
I remember getting caught behind the convent
    turning off the nuns' power.
I remember my first progress report
    with straight A's.

When Dan finished reading, everyone applauded—with good reason. Later, at the break, I asked him if he would type up his poem and send me a copy to share with others. About a week later, I received the poem in the mail, typed in an eighteen-point font and covering three pages. Dan was justly proud of this piece of work.

And here is one of many that I have written along with my students—each one different, each one teaching me new lessons from my life:

About One of My Lives

I was born naked in Nebraska
At the still point, the turning point,
The winter solstice.

I grew up on the farm—the windmill
On the hill stood watch over my days.
Clarice Dodd sat in front of me
In the third grade. I fell in love with
Her pigtails. I once saw limbs and boards
And pieces of machinery fall from the sky
After a tornado passed miles away.
The smell of geraniums will forever
Remind me of my grandmother.
I have heard, after a summer rain,
The air so full of frogs' cries
I could hardly breathe. My father never hugged me,
But when I was twelve, he gave me a newborn calf,
Still wet from birth. I named her Queenie.
Once in June it rained for five days
And the river came crashing to our front door
In the middle of the night.
Sometimes, on summer night, the stars
Came down so close
I could almost walk among them.

Life was a great mystery to me then—
And still.

Since our lives are filled with such moments and memories, you can write autobiographical poems over and over again. Each time, your words will show you amazing things. Each time, your words will teach you to value your amazing life—then and now.

seven

Writing and Healing

new worlds open nothing closes spiraling we move through
lit rooms recovering from wounds skylight heals us believe
just believe faith in all things breathe in the sky and love
sing cry mourn write it all down use everything everything

—ROSLYN, A RECOVERING
BRAIN-TRAUMA PATIENT

Out of Hiding

Roslyn wrote the words in the epigraph above at the end of one of her public writings for our class. It became a kind of anthem of healing for us all. Lynn Brown was in the same writing class with Roslyn. She had her own wounds to heal. One night, as we sat in the Feather Circle sharing writing from our journal work and exploring unhealed wounds, Lynn read to us the following moment from her life:

I remember the coarse itchiness
of the ropes in my hands
and the heat of the metal seat
burning through my shorts as I swung—
suspended between the huge elm branch
and the midwestern dust.
I remember swinging in and out,
up and down,
between cool tree shade and muggy August sun,
I remember trying so hard
to ignore Lou's calling voice.
Instead, I focused on the reassuring rumble
of my Daddy's voice as he droned on
like a lazy summer horsefly.
I remember Lou calling louder,
until finally my Daddy said,
"Be a good girl, Lynn—
go see what your grandfather wants."
I remember leaving the safety of my father's voice
and the haven of the tree swing.
Obediently, I trudged toward the old barn door,
knowing that Lou was waiting for me—
waiting, exposed, in the shadows—
waiting to teach me things
a little girl should not know. . . .

Lynn cried softly as she read. But there was more. Just below this painful revelation on the page, she had also written these few simple words, which she read in a strong voice, like an affirmation:

11-x-8-inch notebook paper,
college ruled,
blue Eraser Mate 2 pen—
these are the tools I use
to mend a tattered life.

Lynn was well on her way to mending her tattered life, to healing her grievous wounds, through the power of her journal writing. And her sharing gave us all permission to bring our own wounds out of hiding and into the "skylight" of healing.

As we do our journal work and come together to share open and honest messages with each other in the form of public writing, we discover one terrible and wonderful truth: We have all been, and we all shall be, wounded by life. There is no choice in the matter. It is an inescapable condition of living. Despite the fairy tales, no one lives happily ever after.

The question is not whether we will be wounded by life. We will be. The question is: How do we respond to our wounding? And, furthermore: What do we do with our wounds? For beyond our wounding lies our power and our salvation. Beyond our wounding, we have choices that are crucial to our health and well-being. We can choose to hide our wounds and pretend and go on bleeding throughout our lives—or we can tell the stories of our wounds, we can "publish" them, and we can heal ourselves. In this way, as Roslyn so beautifully and succinctly tells us, "skylight heals us."

The problem, however, is that we have been taught to do otherwise. We have been trained from birth to hide our wounds. We have been taught that there is something wrong with us if we have been hurt, if we are not living happily ever after. So we do as we have been taught: We hide our wounds in the darkness within us, often hiding them even from ourselves. And in that darkness, with no skylight to heal them, they continue to fester and bleed.

But the problem does not end there, for the hiding of our wounds brings us up against another truth: Ultimately, everything gets published. That is, if I do not say my hurts, do not cry my tears, do not shout my anger, do not tell my stories into the healing skylight of my journal, they will eventually translate themselves into other languages and publish themselves into my very being, into the acts of my life. Hidden and unshared and unhealed, my wounds will slowly translate themselves into a language of illness or alcoholism or abuse or suicide.

In this way, garbage piles on garbage, violence begets violence, abuse victims become abusers, children of alcoholics become alcoholics. The fathers eat sour grapes and the children's teeth are set on edge. In this way, without knowing it, we take on the wounds of our parents, add them to our own wounds, and pass them on to our children.

Toward Healing

Given the tools, we can heal ourselves and break the terrible chain of passing down wounds. Writing is such a tool. By telling our stories—first, to ourselves in our journals and then, if possible, to others in public writing— we can heal ourselves. I see it happen all the time as people do this work, discover this power. And I feel it happen in my life.

I see, for example, how my father was wounded by his parents, disowned because he did not believe as they would have had him believe. And I see how grievously this hurt him and how, having been given no tools for healing, he hid his wounds "like a man," as he had been trained to do, and turned to alcohol. And I see how this, in turn, led to some of my own wounds.

My father needed to tell the stories of his great hurt, so that it could heal. My father needed a journal. Eventually, in a mental hospital, he found Alcoholics Anonymous, where people are encouraged to tell their stories. There he found healing, and he came back to his family.

In my journal work, I have written much about my family's struggles and my father's going to the hospital. As I watch this writing-and-healing process in myself (and in my students), I see it work like medicine, the medicine of skylight. Seeing and saying, I work my way slowly, inch by inch, word by word, toward the healing light. Not long ago, I wrote again in my journal about these things and later shared the following with my class:

More Seeing/More Healing

At eighteen, it was to me
such an un-fatherly, un-manly thing
for you to do—going there.
But it was your wish,
made from where you lay upon the kitchen floor,
made from somewhere beyond
the wine bottle in the brown crumpled sack.
"Take me there," you said as I knelt beside you,
as if you knew at last what must be done.

I remember how green the grounds
the State Hospital that day,
how immaculate it all was,
like some painting I had never seen—
the buildings so white in the June sunlight
they made my eyes water.
We walked you in the door,
Mother and I, afraid to raise our eyes.
I remember the smell of Lysol
and the man with empty eyes
who wanted to tell me about his dog.
We signed some papers I did not understand
and walked with you and the orderly

to your ward. And then we left you there—
I can't remember what we said.
I don't remember if we touched.
I only remember the strange door
with the little barred window
that clanged shut upon your face,
and then you and we were all alone. . . .

At eighteen, I could not understand
what brought you there, my father.
But now, at your age then,
now I think I know. . . .

The world has a way of wearing on us—
they take away our tears and give us toys;
they take away our hearts and give us calculators;
and they tell us one day it will all add up—
but it never does,
and we go on bleeding from our untended wounds.

Even then, even there, you knew that, my father.
Lying on the worn linoleum of that old lost farmhouse,
unable even to get up, you could see at last the lie.

"Take me there," you said. "Take me there"—
and you went away to dance alone
with the King of Hearts.
And then, one day, you came back
to dance with us.

But you and I do not have to wait until our wounds have brought us to such a point as my father reached. We have our journals with us now—and we are writing and healing. One of my students, a middle-aged woman who had never kept a journal before, described the experience this way:

> Would you believe that at one time I actually paid someone to listen to me? It felt really good, but I can't afford it.
>
> I used to tell my cat everything. No matter what I said, she would purr in encouragement. I even cried into her fur like a pillow. Afterwards, she would wash herself and purr. But she died, and I was alone with myself again.
>
> But now I have my journal. Something seems to be happening as I write. I am even meeting the child that used to be me. It all feels like a healing and cleansing process.

EXPLORATION

Scar Stories

Scar stories seem to come easily to us—from childhood to old age, people like to tell stories about their wounds, their operations, their accidents. And Nietzsche tells us that we must "come to love our scars." This Exploration involves looking at your physical scars, your literal wounds, and telling the stories that come with them and need to be told.

Take a few minutes to breathe and quiet yourself.

- **Reflect on your body and the injuries and wounds it has received.**

- **In your journal, draw an outline-sketch of your body.** Do not worry about your artistic ability or accuracy. All you need is a kind of generic representation of your body, like the one I have drawn here:

- **On your drawing, mark the physical wounds and scars you have acquired thus far in your life.** As you do this, you will start remembering things—how each wound happened, how you felt at the time, what you did.

- **Annotate each one.** As you sketch in the scars and wounds you have received, describe briefly how you got each one and what you remember about it.

- **Write freely in your journal about each scar and wound.** Put down all you can remember, without concern for the conventions of public writing. Let the feelings flow from you. If there are parts you cannot remember, dream them, imagine them.

Toward Public Writing

Pick one of your emerging scar stories, one that wants and needs to be told, and begin working it toward a piece of public writing. Perhaps the wounding itself will want to be the center, the heart, of the story, and the drama will unfold around it. Or the wound may serve to illuminate a relationship or help you to see something or someone else more clearly. You never know. Just start telling the story and watch for what unfolds.

Here, for example, is what happened for Beth when she did this Exploration:

And Then I Knew

I could see the panic in his eyes. His lips were moving frantically, but I could not hear what he was saying. My father caught me just as my legs turned to rubber. . . .

It was my own fault. I had wanted so much to help him in those few moments before when I had come strolling through the garage and found him in a jam. He was trying to adjust the tension springs for our garage doors and needed someone to stand on the ladder and hold the handle to the tightly wound metal.

His unwillingness to accept my services only made me more determined to help him. I wanted him to know I was just as tough as my older brothers.

Reluctantly, he explained to me what needed to be done. I mounted the ladder proudly and carefully replaced his hands with my own on the handle that controlled eighty-four pounds of coiled tension. His final instructions to me were to never let up on the pressure that I was applying.

Lulled by surprise and pride at how easy it was to control the force of the coil, I gradually relaxed my concentration. Suddenly, the coil leaped wildly out of my control. The handle whirled ferociously, biting at me and throwing me from the ladder to the concrete below.

My father was there in an instant. He held me as my legs gave out and quickly wrapped a cloth around my finger where the bone was sticking out.

The softness and gentleness on his face as he cared for me is something I will never forget. He had often told me that he loved me, but from then on I knew how much he really did—and still does.

Notice how Beth lets her story begin after the wounding and then flashes back to bring the reader up to that point. Observe how she shows rather than tells. Note how she does not overdramatize but, if anything, downplays the wounding ("quickly wrapped a cloth around my finger where the bone was sticking out"). Also, Beth uses simple but powerful words: "the coil leaped wildly," "the handle whirled . . . biting at me," "he held me as my legs gave out." This is a strong piece of public writing. It started with Beth's scar annotation, grew in her journal writing, and gradually took form as she worked and reworked it for others to see and feel.

This is the writing process. This is where public writing comes from, gradually emerging from within you, from within your heart, and finding its form. Let your scar stories evolve in this way.

EXPLORATION

Heart Scars

Heart scars are a variation on literal scars, but these stories do not come forth so readily. Here you will explore your emotional wounds and begin to tell the stories you may have been trained to hide from yourself and from others. These are stories that need to be told.

Begin by breathing and quieting yourself. As always, go slowly, look carefully, respect the process.

- **Reflect on your emotional wounds.** What are the hurts, the traumas of your heart? Look for those wounds that did not bleed, but often hurt more than the wounds that did.

- **Draw a picture of a heart and mark your wounds on it.** Some of these scars will be major and obvious ("my parents' divorce," "my brother's death," "Sarah's suicide," and so on). Others will be smaller and more subtle ("jilted by Clarice in the third grade," "had to have my dog Shana put to sleep," "got kicked off the swimming team my senior year," and so on). Put them all on your heart as you remember them.

- **In your journal, write about your scars and wounds.** Pick the ones that you feel a need to work with. Explore them. Wonder about them. Feel them again. Some of them may not yet be scars but may still be raw and unhealed hurts. This is a sign that you need to work with them, to tell the stories of their happening, to heal them.

Toward Public Writing

Pick one of your heart scars and work it into a piece of public writing. Sharing your stories not only helps you but helps others, giving them permission and an example to follow in telling the stories of their own wounds, to begin their own healing.

A year or so ago, as we were doing this Exploration in one of my writing classes, a student named Doris handed me a scrap of paper with the words "I cannot do this" hastily scrawled on it, and left the room. I followed her into the hallway where, with tears in her eyes, she told me the Exploration was too painful. She said it brought back terrible memories of being abused by her mother, which she could not deal with. I told Doris it was all right, that she would deal with this still painful wound when she was ready, and not to worry about the Exploration. I suggested she go for a walk and breathe and enjoy the day.

At our gathering the next week, Doris shared with us a small piece from her journal writing about this great wound from her past. Supported and encouraged by the other class members, she continued this journal work, this healing work, over the next few weeks. In fact, she did this work so well, she so healed herself from this wounding, that she recently was able to read the following poem to 350 eighth-graders at a school assembly where we had been invited to share our writing:

The Shadow Monsters

I live in a tiny, dark room
trapped by my innocence and size
I cling to a tattered quilt
of so many faded patches

my cot presses
against my parents' bed
a hundred grayish shadows
reach across the ceiling
smothering the walls and floor

my five-year-old mind
remembers those nights
remembers the darkness and shadowed walls
where the deep, dark corners held
see-through monsters with mercury eyes
transparent claws and silvery scissor-sharp teeth
who tirelessly watched me, waited
and watched me more

but these monsters never, ever
jumped on me,
tore my arms off or
ripped out my tongue
they waited
like me
for the scariest
most dangerous one
the monster who could make the door move. . . .

And every night, the She monster would come
She moved the door open

and I,
the cornered prey,
lay tense and still
the light would push in
and fall across
my scrunched-up face
the monster stared hard and long
searching for any clue that
I was not asleep
I couldn't keep my eyelids still
so she dragged me by my hair
or hit me with brushes and hangers
or whatever would hurt

my screams never stopped the shadow monsters
nor stopped Her endless reign
I remember telling God

You can leave the shadow monsters
but please send my mother away.

This is the healing work you will do, the freeing work, in turning your journal writing into public writing. Your writings will become gifts to yourself and others. Let this woman's courageous sharing help you as you do your own work.

EXPLORATION

Memories That Sustain Us

Sustain: "To keep in existence; maintain . . . To supply with necessities or nourishment . . . To support from below; keep from falling or sinking . . . To support the spirits, vitality; to encourage . . ." —*American Heritage Dictionary*

Much of our work on our own history focuses upon healing wounds and exorcising monsters from out past. But we also find gifts of sustenance—moments and memories that sustain us. These are memories of special places and special times that we can go back to in our minds and in our journals. They include: memories of home and roots; memories of little lessons learned; remembered acts of courage or caring by others that light our way; special moments of insight or understanding; little epiphanies lost in our consciousness, waiting for us to reclaim their sustenance; and on and on.

Be still with your journal now and focus on sustaining memories and moments from your life.

- **Let your mind drift back to small, meaningful moments.** Remember sustaining memories from your childhood (your father's tear-stained face as you lay in the hospital bed, your hiding place among the whispering leaves of the cottonwood tree, the time your mother hugged you in the principal's office, that fishing trip with your brother).

- **Look carefully for memories that are within you.** Find memories that make you smile, memories that, perhaps, have been sustaining you from beneath your awareness without your even knowing that you knew.

- **Bring these memories to the surface now and collect them in your journal.** As you write them in your journal, more details will come floating to the surface of your memory. Add to them. Let them grow.

Toward Public Writing

Pick one sustaining memory that has emerged for you in your journal writing and begin moving it into a public form. Work with it until it begins to find a fitting shape—perhaps in the form of a poem or a short narrative piece.

As always, this is a good chance to work on showing rather than telling. Let your readers feel the sustenance of this memory for themselves through the power and the focus of your words. Try to get your words to show your readers what happened and how it felt—just as Lisa, a young Lakota woman in my class, did so effectively with this memory from her childhood:

Rainwater Walking

Once I ran away when I was ten. I only got as far as the skinny creek a hundred yards away. I stayed there and waited for Grams to come after me. She never let harm touch us.

I waited there under the pine tree by the creek—and eventually she came, as I knew she would. I remember seeing her short, round body slowly making its way down the tree-covered hill to the creek. When she saw me, she said she came to get rainwater from the creek because it was good for her plants. But I knew why she came.

Grams came to listen to why I ran away. I had been arguing with my sister again—and to me the fights always seemed like the end of the world.

Grams asked me to walk with her. We slowly moved along, listening to what each of us had to say. The gnarly little oak trees watched and talked to us with their faded green leaves. We eventually ended up back at our little white house. By then I had forgotten why I ran away—and Grams never did get her rainwater.

And here is one that I wrote a few years ago, one that is even more precious to me now that my mother is gone:

My Mother's Love

When I was growing up, I was trained to be a man. My father was my model and all the things I did were manly things—hunting, working in the fields, playing football and basketball and baseball. But now, years later, as I go through life struggling to survive and find meaning, more often the memories of my mother's quiet and unselfish love are what sustain me. Here is one memory of her that lies deep within me.

My mother had just been wheeled back from the recovery room after having surgery for cancer. The surgeon had ravaged her body, hacking the cancer cells from her with his scalpel. I had flown back from Arizona to the hospital in Lincoln and was the first to enter her hospital room. She lay like death, blasted by trauma and anesthetic. I could see how near was the skull beneath the skin, how thin the line between life and death. For a long while, I sat beside her, crying softly, holding her hand. And then, at last, she opened her eyes and came back a bit from the edge of death. Somehow, she knew what had been done to her, knew that her body was butchered. But even then, in her great love, her concern was for me. Her first words were for my comfort, as softly she whispered: "It is late. I am all right. Go find a place to sleep. You need your rest."

Such love as this still amazes me—and blesses me—and goes with me wherever I go.

As we collect such memories in our journals, and as we turn them into public writing to acknowledge them and share them, their sustenance grows. As you go along now in your writing and being, continue to collect and share such memories as they come to you. And they will continue to sustain you.

eight

Seeking Community

Namasté: I honor the place in you in which the entire universe dwells. I honor the place in you which is of love, of truth, of light, of peace. When you are in that place in you, and I am in that place in me, we are one.

—"NAMASTÉ" IS A HINDU GREETING
ACKNOWLEDGING THE TRUE
COMMUNITY OF SELVES.

Another World

The poet e.e. cummings once told an aspiring writer that to be "nobody-but-yourself" in a world that is doing its best to make you "everybody else" means to fight the hardest battle that any human being can fight. As we do this writing-and-being work, that is what we are doing: fighting to uncover who we really are beneath the masks and the training and the expectations.

This struggle to find ourselves and love ourselves is one we must undertake. No one can do this work for us. As I pointed out in Chapter 1, when we began this journey, being alone is an important part of the commitment to the writing-and-being process. Aloneness is essential to finding our own voice in a society that is always calling us away from ourselves, always telling us the answers are out there somewhere.

At first, this process may seem frightening and lonely. When I began to keep a journal, to talk to myself, to write openly and honestly from my heart, I often felt very much alone. Not only did I have to write alone, but I also found myself growing increasingly unwilling to tolerate the often superficial and competitive groups where I had before sought acceptance and community.

My values began to change. My world began to change. Here is a little story, moved from my journal, that shows those shifting values in my life.

Accidental Tourist at the Grand Canyon

Last Friday, I called Ed Brown in Berkeley, the director of the National Writing Project. I was still high on the power of the readings/sharings my Native American students had done at local high schools over the past two weeks. I thought: I will be attending the National Council of Teachers of English conference in Pittsburgh in two weeks. Five of my Native American students will do a presentation for the conference. Since the directors of Writing Projects from across the country will be meeting for two days at the same time, why not offer my students to do a reading or opening ceremony or something? So I called and left a message for Ed. Later in the day, he called back; our conversation went something like this:

ED: I got your message. Something about your students doing a reading or something for the meetings?

ME: Well, I have this group of Native American students who do readings of their personal stories and cultural presentations. . . . Five of them will be there with me. I just thought if you wanted them to do an opening reading or something. . . . There is one man in the group, he's Sioux from South Dakota, who drums and sings in his native language. . . . [Alvis could do a powerful blessing ceremony to get the program started right, but I did not get a chance to explain further. . . .]

ED: Well, let's see . . . . We just finished printing the program this morning . . . . Everything is pretty well set . . . not much room for anything else. . . .

ME: Hey, no problem. I understand. Just wanted to offer, in case we could help in any way. . . .

ED: Well, wait a minute. Let me see here. How about this? On Friday evening we are having an open-bar cocktail time— perhaps your student could sing and play in the background.

There was a long pause as I gazed at a chasm the size of the Grand Canyon that lay between us and tried to think of something to say. Finally, I mutter something about that probably not being appropriate, thank you anyway, and hung up.

Days later, I cannot shake a vague, sad image I am left with. Alvis is a gentle, middle-aged man who looks as if he stepped right out of *Dances with Wolves*. He has had a hard life, and he is studying for his elementary education degree so he can work with children. Last week at Mesa High School, I watched him stand at the front of a small auditorium and tell 200 or so students about his life. Then he read a piece he had written about his friend who came back from Vietnam and "drank Orange Rock wine like Kool-Aid and just wasn't the same." He told how his friend nearly drank himself to death but eventually "heard the eagle-bone whistle and found the Sun Dance ceremony," and how Alvis himself learned to sing the "Vietnam Veterans' Song" the proper way—sober.

Then, Alvis leaned down and began to thump the table in front of him in the steady, ancient beat of the drum. And in the high-pitched, wailing, traditional Dakota Sioux way, he sang the "Vietnam Veterans' Song" of a thousand powwows and ceremonies. And 200 adolescents, brutalized and desensitized by the likes of Andrew Dice Clay and Howard Stern and Demolition Man and Beavis and Butthead and a thousand crude and arrogant singers and standup comedians and pop-culture stars, listened in rapt silence . . . and applauded when he finished.

So I shake myself, shedding the image of Alvis sitting in a cocktail bar singing sacred Dakota songs "in the background" as convention-goers in three-piece suits and cocktail dresses quote Shakespeare and tell jokes and talk politics.

Sorry, Mr. Brown, I can't cross the Canyon. There is another world over here on the North Rim, and I'm afraid I haven't conveyed it to you. I will try again. But for now I'm staying with Alvis.

As I have gone further into this seemingly solitary writing work, two things have changed what at first looked like a lonely endeavor. First, I began to care for myself, to value time with myself, to find meaningful community with myself, so that being alone no longer meant being lonely. And second, as the story suggests, I began reaching out to others on a deeper and more loving level.

Knocking on the Door of Community

Outwardly, then, this writing process looks isolated and perhaps even selfish and narcissistic—just us alone with our journals, talking to ourselves. But if we take the steps carefully and honestly, a wonderful reciprocity can grow: As we reach inward toward our Selves, we begin to reach outward toward others, toward the world at large. But we reach out not in quite the same way as before—not in judgment or competition, not in a grasping way, but with open eyes and a caring heart.

Thus, as we tell our stories and come to care for our Selves, we find, to our great joy, that we are less alone than ever before. We find that others, too, are wounded and struggling, and we reach out to each other in ways that were not possible before, when we were hiding and pretending. We begin inevitably to care for others, for everything. Followed fully, then, the solitary writing process becomes a caring, communal, and spiritual process.

Sadly, much of our coming together in this society is still shaped by old and false equations between our outer struggles and our inner value. Belonging to groups is often based on some degree of exclusivity and elitism (i.e., leaving others out). Many communities unwittingly promote pretending, dishonesty, and suppressing feelings. In this way, by their very nature, they drain energy and exclude the power of true communion.

It usually goes like this: I ask to join your group. You ask to see my résumé. You want to see if I am good enough, to see if I am worthy of belonging, to see if I am a prince and not a frog. If you accept me, it is not really me you accept. It is this pretense of me, this image, this act. And so whenever we come together, I must pretend to be something I am not so that I may continue to "belong." I must hide my wounds, my warts, my frogness. I must pretend to be a prince in the hope that you will accept me. This pretending takes all my energy, all my spontaneity, all my creativity.

There are alternatives to the deadly pretending with each other, and we begin to find them as we find our Selves through the solitary work in our journals. True communities are possible. I gradually came to realize this through attending occasional Alcoholics Anonymous meetings with my father. I would spend a couple of hours with a bunch of "failures" as they struggled to straighten out their lives, and I would come away feeling oddly energized and spiritually uplifted.

"What is going on here?" I wondered. And I watched. Slowly, I realized that AA is one of the few communities within our society where we do not have to hide and pretend in order to be accepted. There are gatherings where we can give each other energy, where we can come together and be healthy for each other, where we can help each other to survive and grow.

When you knock on the door of AA, for example, you do not get in by telling those inside how wonderful you are, by showing them your glowing résumé, by convincing them you are worthy because you are unwounded. Rather, you knock on the door and say, "Help me, for I am hurting; I am struggling; I am not perfect; I am not a prince; and above all, I cannot make it alone." The members of this group, who are also wounded, open their arms and welcome you into the possibility of true community and shared love and energy.

After seeing how AA works to heal those in its circle and how powerful it is, I hungered for such communities. For a while, I even considered becoming an alcoholic so I could belong to AA, but I was afraid I might fail. I wondered: Why does it seem we have to become alcoholics or drug addicts or have mental breakdowns or attempt suicide before we can come together as whole people, without pretense, before we can speak from our hearts and tell our stories to each other?

So a small courage grew in me. I experimented with making my classes and workshops—and all my relationships—more like AA and less like the usual social meetings. You can do this, too—and you will begin to feel the difference, the love-energy. It begins in your journal, where you come together in true community with yourself and write honestly and openly, where you give yourself permission to acknowledge your pain and sadness and fear, where you begin to accept and love yourself as you are, without pretense.

Then this love-energy can move outward into your community with others, into a world where you do not have to compete or one-up anyone, because you are grasping for nothing, because you are centered in the peace of your Self. From there, you can reach out to others in love and acceptance. There, together, all of you can share, not your grand achievements and your shining résumés, but your scars and your pain and your fears and your small joys—your tears and your laughter and your love.

Developing a Kind and Supportive Writing Group

Based upon the above beliefs and our innate aversion to the often mean-spirited "chop-shop" writing groups fostered in many creative writing departments, my friends and I have developed a simple, helpful, and kindlier approach to helping each other work on our writing and being. In my writing classes and workshops, for example, I put the writers (including myself) in small groups of four or five. (If you aren't in a class, you can easily do this on your own: Just find three or four other writers who want to write and work with you.) I lead the students into some focused journal work in class in much the same manner of the Explorations in this book. The instructions are then to keep working for the next few days with what we have started on in our journals—and to return to class with an emerging piece of public writing, with copies for each person in our small group.

I encourage the students to bring a piece they have worked hard on, a piece that is clean and readable, a piece that they are ready to test out on the trial audience of their writing groups; and I, of course, do the same.

When we gather in our writing groups, we follow carefully this procedure:

The first writer to go passes out hard copies of his or her work to each person in the group. Then, while that writer reads the piece aloud, clearly and carefully, the others follow along on the hard copy, making notes. Basically, they are looking for three fairly simple things, which include:

- elements that, as readers, "work" for them, positive aspects—anything from a word choice to a way of describing something to a sharing that resonates with their own experience;

- questions they have about the piece, places where they are confused or sentences or words that are not clear—any things that, as readers, leaves them puzzled or unclear;

- suggestions to make the piece better, stronger, clearer.

As the writer reads his piece aloud, the others are looking for and making simple notes in relation to the above three things.

After the writer has finished reading, and when the others are ready, he or she reads it aloud a second time. This second reading is important because, having been through it once, the group members now have a second chance to attend to and make notes about the their three response areas.

After the second reading, the group members take turns responding and giving feedback in each of the three areas, always beginning with the positive, with what works for them in the piece. (The writer now listens and makes notes on his or her own copy, notes toward revision based upon this test audience.)

After each member has shared their positive responses to the piece, then they each have a chance to ask the writer questions about places where they were confused or unclear. Often, in the process of responding to their questions, the writer will readily see things he or she needs to change or clarify.

Finally, after questions, the readers take turns making suggestions. Always, these are made only as suggestions, not as "should's." Always, these are phrased in helpful, supportive tones: "Could you put an example in at that point to help the reader see?," "Have you thought about doing this whole piece in present tense?," "What about using a word like . . . ?"

After the group has finished responding in each of these three areas, the writer then has a chance to ask them for help or advice on any other issues he or she wants feedback on. Then they go on to the next piece and repeat the procedure in support of that writer.

All this is done in a tone of support and encouragement—we are like midwives, helping this piece to get born. And all three ways of responding can be done by anyone, anyone who is a caring and perceptive reader-listener. You don't have to be any kind of expert or have a Ph.D. in English to share what works for you, what confuses you, and what suggestions you might have to help me with my piece.

Notice, too, that none of this involves "editing," which is often the sole focus of some so-called writing groups. Editing—checking spelling, grammar, punctuation, etc.—comes last, after the piece is finished. You can be an editing group for each other, when the time is right and the piece has found its form. But before that, you have much more important work to do.

Leaving behind egos and expertise and focusing on helping the writer and the writing, we become partners in this creative process. In this way, often after our class or workshop has ended, writing groups choose to continue working together, writing together.

One student, looking back on her work in her writing group and her subsequent sharing with the class, described our time together this way:

Here in this room together, I have told you stories from my life that I have told no one before, not even myself. And you have not shunned me nor run away from me. Indeed, many of you even cried with me as I read these stories (no one has ever done that for me before) and you wrote me notes thanking me and you reached out to me as though I had given you some great gift. And you told the stories of your own wounds to me, and here in the circle I was no longer alone in the world. Here in this room together, telling our stories from our hearts, we became brothers and sisters.

Thus, as we do this seemingly solitary journal work, and then move our words outward to our writing groups and to our classes and to the world, we become more deeply connected and less alone than ever before. It is a journey toward love. And when we meet each other on that journey, we smile and say, "Namasté."

EXPLORATION

Reaching In, Reaching Out

As you reach inward through your writing, you will inevitably find yourself reaching outward to other people. You will become more sensitive to the nature of your interactions. This Exploration is a tangible way to attend to community in your life.

Breathe deeply for a few minutes and quiet yourself.

- **In your mind's eye, review the interactions of your day.** Focus on the people you interacted with. Look carefully at your contacts with individuals, your group gatherings, your chance meetings.

Notice your feelings in relation to each interaction. Sense the changes in your energy level that occurred with each encounter.

- **In your journal, make a list of contacts and interactions with others in your day that stand out.** List each one briefly, simply noting who it was with and the circumstances and perhaps a note about what happened and how you felt.

- **Go down your list and reflect on each interaction listed.** Look closely at how each interaction left you feeling: Did it seem to give you energy or take energy away from you?

- **Write in your journal about each encounter.** Wonder why some contacts with others left a positive feeling and others a negative feeling. Look closely at any contacts you had with children or animals. Wonder about the source of the differences in your feelings. Look closely at whether you felt centered and at ease in your Self or whether you felt the need to pretend.

Do this kind of observing and exploring frequently in your journal. You might want to do this Exploration focusing on three major "interaction areas" in your life: your home (your living place); your job (your workplace or school place); your friends (your chosen social places). This Exploration can be very revealing and can lead to new choices and changes in your life.

As you do this work, you will realize that you can choose to have positive communities in your life. You will find yourself wanting to make your close relationships healthier and more positive. You will find yourself valuing a workplace where people treat each other with dignity and respect. You will find yourself seeking out people who are energy givers rather than energy takers. And, inevitably, as you do this work, you will become an energy giver.

Toward Public Writing

Pick one of the interactions you wrote about in your journal and work it into a piece of public writing, a scene that brings out the positive or negative energy you felt. Do not tell it; rather, get the action, dialogue, word choice, and imagery to show it so that the reader feels what you felt.

Experiment with forms, styles, and points of view. You could approach this assignment as a descriptive scene or write it wholly in dialogue. The obvious way to relate this story would be in your voice in first person. But you might try doing it in third person, seeing yourself as one of the characters in this little drama. Or tell it in first person from the other person's point of view.

Do not be afraid to juggle and fictionalize the facts in order to bring out the emotional truth of the incident. As always, as you turn this into a piece of public writing, you will continue to learn from it. You will continue to understand it and yourself better. That is almost invariably the case when you work with real material that comes from inside you. You get a double payoff: Your public writing gets stronger *and* your personal understanding grows.

Here are two small pieces that emerged from watching my interactions:

4/17—Monday—San Francisco (Negative Energy)

After my morning presentation to teachers, I have a few hours before I catch the shuttle to the airport. So I leave the lavish hotel and go out to walk the streets of San Francisco. I return in less than an hour, unnerved and upset. The visions that I had seen through the shuttle windows coming in last night had not, after all, been some weird, surrealistic illusions of my tired mind. . . .

The streets are teeming with a wild jumble of people. Businessmen in $500 suits step around filthy human bodies lying on sidewalks. Just across the street from the hotel, I walk past a sad, window-boarded building with a marquee advertising "24-HOUR NUDE DANCING." A city bus rounds a corner and smashes down a saw-horse barricade over a newly poured cement patch—without even slowing down. Desolate men with dirty stocking caps pulled down tightly poke languidly in garbage cans or sit in doorways smoking cigarettes. They have eyes like smashed-out windows. . . .

Later, getting ready to check out of the hotel, I look down from my window on the twenty-second floor into these canyons of misery. The people are small and far away, their movements like ants. But a strange soaring catches my eye. And then another. Seagulls have come in from the ocean to ride the currents between the skyscrapers, to ply with grace these canyons of misery.

4/18—Tuesday—ASU (Positive Energy)

Fifteen dark-eyed guests—high school students from Ok Chin Reservation School—file in to join the twenty-four students in my Native American writing class. Kathy, their counselor, is with them. She and I hug. I welcome the guests and ask my students to tell about the writing projects they are working on. We go around the room; each student speaks shyly but sincerely. As they talk, I notice that Lee's little baby, Sirus, wrapped in a blanket, is being passed around the room like an eagle feather in a Feather Circle. Even some of the visitors take a turn holding him. Left-brain dividing lines begin to melt. For a little while, I feel myself dissolving. For a little while, the room grows fuzzy and fills with love and hope.

EXPLORATION

Acts of Love

Mother Teresa once said that people can do no great things, only "small things with great love." Your days are filled with opportunities to do small things with great love. Your days also bring you gifts of love from others. You only need to look. You only need to focus on them, and they will grow and fill your days. This Exploration will help you recognize opportunities to give and receive love.

Breathe deeply and quiet yourself. Touch that center within yourself where love lives.

- **In your mind, look back over your day for acts of love.** Look for kindnesses both given and received. Look carefully. Often these moments are eclipsed by more blatant events. Often they are in disguise, so be patient and let them appear to you.

- **Take five minutes and list briefly in your journal kindnesses you received from others this day.**

- **Take another five minutes and list kindnesses you did for others this day.**

- **Describe at least one kindness you did for yourself this day.** This one is tricky. Wonder about it. Look closely.

- **Make a wish list of acts of caring in your journal.** Include any act of caring—for others, for yourself, for the world. Do not be limited by what seems possible. List things you would do, could do, if you were not constrained by other demands. Let your imagination play with your wishes, but make them specific. List them down the page in the form of phrases, such as:

- *Meditate with Willow-Cat every morning.*
- *Call my mother in the middle of the day, and ask her to tell me that childhood story again.*
- *Get a sweet potato, put it in water, and watch for miracles.*
- *Play hooky with Jimmie and take him to a Cubs game.*

Toward Public Writing

Write a brief lead-in or introduction to the list of acts of caring you made in the "Acts of Love" Exploration. Say something about how you are feeling or what you are needing in your life now, so that the introduction leads into a wish list of acts of caring for yourself and for others. Then pick out some items from your list that feel good, and weave them together into a wish list poem for the world.

Here, for example, is a piece that happened for me once when I did this Exploration with my class:

And the Little Leaves Rose Up

A few years ago, the doctor (in his small knowing) took his scalpel and cut my thyroid gland (wondrous thoracic butterfly) out of my throat. When I awakened, he looked grim and uttered words like "carcinoma" and "malignant."

The earth trembled then. I stood up, eyes wide. Skyscrapers fell—and little leaves rose up and blossomed.

Ever after, things that matter have been mostly things of love. And always, the little leaves keep reminding me:

to listen to the lessons of Angel's eyes;
to seek silence daily like a lover;

to hug my daughters
(while they are awake)
and to touch my Lorrie softly
(while she sleeps);
to check the pulse
of all those dear to me
and those who are becoming so;
to wear my love easily,
like old Levis,
and to invest in it daily—
not fretting the stocks and bonds
that I do not understand;
to cry deeply (tears do not compute)
and to laugh freely (nor does laughter);
to love God as if I believed in Her,
and my neighbor, too;
to lament my lost and ludicrous children
and to find them daily;
to go naked into the river. . . .

As always, do not be locked into the form or the example. Play with the idea and see what happens for you. Just let it lead you outward, in love, to the world.

EXPLORATION

Random Acts of Kindness

Sometime during every semester, I like to assign this Exploration to myself and my students because it asks us to behave deliberately in a certain way and to watch, write about, and learn from what happens.

The assignment goes like this: For the next week, you are to practice little random acts of kindness—dozens of them in all kinds of situations. These can be anything helpful to anyone else, from giving a flower to a stranger or helping a young mother get her baby's stroller off the bus to simply stopping to say good morning to the bag lady on the street.

- **Watch for opportunities as you go about your daily life.**

- **Be spontaneous and creative and genuine with your kindnesses, and see what happens.**

- **Watch carefully as you do these acts.** Observe as if you are watching a play and you don't know what is going to happen. Watch your feelings, your reactions. Watch what the other person does, how the other person responds.

- **Then, as soon as you can, sit down quietly with your journal and record in detail what happened.** Write about what you did, how the other person responded, how you felt. Tell the story of that little encounter.

- **Do this several times in different situations over the course of a few days.**

Toward Public Writing

Now, take one of these encounters and work it into a piece of public writing. Pick one that surprised you with its outcome, one that taught you something, or one that felt particularly good or particularly awkward to you.

Play around with the form this piece wants or needs to take as you work on it. Try telling it in first person or in third person, or in the form of a script for a short play. See what form feels best as you work this into a piece of writing to share with others. See what you continue to learn from it as you work on it. Give it a title.

Then pick another one and see what happens as you work on it.

Here, for example, is a short but surprising account of a random act of kindness by one of my students:

Do unto Others

"I hope you like it. It's Heath Bar Crunch   one of my favorites," I said as I handed him the plastic spoon and the pint of Ben and Jerry's ice cream.

I had never been this close to him, and for the first time in the three years that I had seen him on this campus, he was silent. I didn't stay to watch him eat it—and, in fact, I was surprised he even took it.

As I walked away, I smiled and thought to myself this was probably one of the rare times that the screaming, Bible-thumping preacher on the mall was greeted with something other than a nasty look or an obscenity or a raised middle finger.

And here is Pam's account of one of her acts of kindness—one that, as life will often do, turned around and surprised her:

Kindness for Dummies

I was exiting an office building when I observed a man trying to get out of his car and into his wheelchair. I rushed over and asked if I could help. He politely said, "No, thank you"—but thinking he just didn't want to bother me, I insisted.

I struggled to pull the chair the rest of the way out of his car and then spent awhile trying to unfold it. I rolled it as close to him as I could. He used all of his upper-body strength to maneuver himself into the chair. He thanked me. I told him it was my pleasure and wished him a good day.

As I walked to my car, I felt a cheerful sense of accomplishment from being able to help this person. When I reached my car, however, I looked back and saw that he was now getting back into his car. I then realized that I had just helped him get out of a car that he was trying to get into. Not only that, but from start to finish it took him about forty-five seconds for this procedure. When I helped him, it took us about five minutes.

I then realized that he was the one who had done the act of kindness, fulfilling my need rather than his own. I felt very foolish—and yet I had to smile as I drove away.

This random kindness Exploration is a good one to practice often. It may well lead to some meaningful and instructive writing for yourself and others—and even if it doesn't, the world will be better for your having done it.

nine

Taking Back Our Hearts

As a child in kindergarten, I drew freely on a scribble-pad of newsprint, stories from my heart. . . . I had another language then, a language of caring. Now, as a college student, I write freely in a journal, just like the scribble-pad I had in kindergarten. I write stories from my heart, trying to survive.

—BRYAN, A NAVAJO STUDENT IN MY
RAINBOW SECTION WRITING CLASS

The Feather Circle

I moved to Arizona more than fifteen years ago. I came here after four years of the intellectual, left-brained rigors of graduate school in Nebraska. Beyond my approved study of sonnets and semicolons, however, I had been secretly reading about New Physics and brain research and Pirsig's *Zen and the Art of Motorcycle Maintenance* and hungering for much more than graduate school had fed me.

In Buddhist terms, I was ready for the teacher. And my teachers came. If I had not been so hungry, I could easily have missed them. They were the occasional silent shadows among the noisy Anglo whiteness of my classes. They were the dark-eyed, tattered remnants of the genocide that began American history. They were strangers in their own sacred land. They were Native Americans.

They have taught me well over the years. What I have learned from them, I use in all my classes—and in the very heartbeat of my life. So what I share here is not about Native Americans and writing. It is about all of us, about our writing and our being. It is about taking back a part of ourselves that has been lost, a part without which none of us can either write well or be well. It is about taking back our hearts.

Sometime during my first year of teaching here, one of my Native American students shared with me a common saying among his people: "When you leave the reservation and go away to school, you have to leave your heart behind." Isn't that the truth, for all of us? I sighed, remembering the years of memorization of sterile facts; remembering all the heartless, bloodless, meaningless, critical analyses and expository essays; remembering being taught not to use the first-person pronoun in formal writing.

Not long after this early lesson, I was introduced to the Feather Circle. Many variations of the Feather Circle or Talking Circle exist among Native American tribes, and I do not pretend to know about them all. But I have experienced one powerful common denominator, whether the circle is held in the hogan or the tipi or the sweat lodge or the condominium or the classroom: When it is your turn to speak, when the eagle feather is passed to you and you hold it in your hand, you are encouraged to speak from your heart.

Speak from your heart. That is all. Yet that simple dictum sends the blood of life pumping through empty skeletons of words and lives and restores the possibility of using language as an instrument of creation.

Sitting in the sweat lodge and the Feather Circle, I have been touched and helped and healed by the powerful words emanating from that simple suggestion, far beyond the healing I have found in any orthodox language class.

Warriors of the Rainbow

With such experiences in my heart, five years ago I began teaching a section of first-year composition exclusively for Native American students. My overt rationale was that, properly envisioned, a writing class would be a natural place to give these students a sense of community and help them survive as strangers in a strange land of 40,000 students at Arizona State University. My deeper motivation was that I wanted to go on learning from the Native American culture, and I wanted to use the Feather Circle as the guiding metaphor for the classroom and for our writing in the class.

The students and I decided to call our class the "Rainbow Section." In any given semester, it is one of more than a hundred sections of first-year composition at the university. The *ASU Course Bulletin* does not say "Rainbow Section"; it just lists another "First-Year Comp" class like all the rest. There is, however, a footnote saying, "For Native American students only." That is but the beginning of its uniqueness.

We call our class the "Rainbow Section" after the Native American prophecy that says:

When the Earth is sick and dying, all over the world people will rise up as warriors of the rainbow to save the planet.

This "rising up," we believe, must begin in our own hearts and grow from our caring and understanding. And somehow, language—not modern, manipulative, Madison Avenue language or the sterile language of the textbook, but authentic, careful, "I-Thou" language—is a part of this work, a tool for all rainbow warriors to use to help save themselves and save the planet.

Speaking of such things in a freshman composition class, of course, makes us mavericks. Still, we cannot help but look out the window and see that the Earth is dying and that human beings and their words have gone astray—and that somehow the two are connected.

In the Rainbow Section, as in the traditional Native American Feather Circle, we speak openly and honestly. We do not look for our words in the library; we try to find them in our hearts. We write to ourselves in our journals ("How do I know what I know till I see what I say?") before we write to the world. We seek our own voices—not Shakespeare's or Hemingway's or Faulkner's, but our own. We use our words to find out who we are and what really matters in this world. And in doing this, we often arrive at a place far from where the commercials and the textbooks and the school administration would lead us.

Then, as we work the words from our hearts and our journals into public writings to share with others, we let the words seek a form. We let the form arise from the words themselves. We remember that, as a baby grows in its mother's womb, the heart grows first and all else comes from that. We remember that a heart can grow a skeleton, but a skeleton cannot grow a heart. We start, always, with the heart.

While it may seem that we do not care much about "rhetoric" and "modes of composition" and such things studied in more orthodox writing classes down the hall, do not be deceived. It is just that we want our words to take shape like the clay in the potter's hands, like the wool in the weaving. We want them to hold up in the world outside the classroom. We want to be able to take our words home with us. We want them to help us survive and grow. We want to feel our words as instruments of creation. We want them to be alive with our own living and loving—and to help others to live and love.

Native Images

Without our ever intending it to happen, a group called "Native Images" emerged from the Rainbow Section. Writing by members of Native Images has touched hundreds of people of all ages and backgrounds. In the second year of the Rainbow Section, a teacher friend at a local high school brought his American literature class to visit my Native American class one morning in October. Hesitantly, my students read some of their writing and shared bits of themselves and their culture with the visiting students. It was a simple, powerful learning experience for everyone involved, a Feather Circle without the feather, and the beginning of much more to come.

Other teachers heard about what my students had done, and I began getting requests to bring them to classrooms at ASU and surrounding community schools. My students gradually became more confident about reading their writing, and the dimensions of our sharings grew. One student put together a slide-tape presentation about his homeland on the reservation, which we incorporated into our sharings. Others drummed and sang spiritual songs in their native language. But the focus of our sharings remained (and still remains) in the reading of the students' words from their hearts.

Two years ago, Native Images became both an official campus organization and an advanced writing and community outreach class. In these two years, we have done more than a hundred presentations for classes, conferences, church services, and workshops. The Native American writers have shared their work and their hearts with audiences ranging from 350 seventh- and eighth-graders at an inner-city school assembly to classes on reservations to inmates at Arizona State Prison.

Last spring, we published a collection of their writing and artwork called *The Heart's Vision*. The title comes from a piece called "Emergence," written by Rutherford Ashley, a Navajo student:

I see them all
with the heart's vision—
the one that never forgets feathery afternoon clouds
the one that reminds us that life starts gently,
like the small candle flame, a whisper

    I feel them
    like the warmth of fire
    I hear them
    like the trembling of nighttime elms

This scape is warm
and eternal
like sand
and wind
It is here they stand
in great numbers
    some giggle
    and smile with chapped cheeks
    some stand
    aged and grey-haired
    with warm stories they can point to
    like oily secrets revealed by strands of sage
    some circle overhead
    and some leave four-legged tracks in the snow

They, my family,
all stand
in great numbers
within my heart

    and within their hearts
    stand many more

My students go on amazing me and teaching me. And down the hall in other rooms, other students are writing in the "modes of rhetoric"— they are writing serialization papers and comparison papers and classification papers. They are learning to make proper skeletons in their English classes, for their English classes. I do not doubt that this is a good thing to do, but still I wonder: Do they take their words home with them? Do their words help them toward peace, toward love? Do their words reach out to others? And I think of the line from Arlene's poem to her mother about being sent away to boarding school: "You did not know they would take away my songs and my prayers."

We cannot live by the left brain alone. Language is not a subject in school. Language is a miracle, a gift given to us as much for songs and prayers as for expository essays. More than ever, we need the power of language as an instrument of creation.

The Feather Circle has become the central metaphor for all my writing classes, Native American or not. I have come to see the Feather Circle as a series of concentric circles, beginning with writers writing alone in their journal, writing from their hearts. The next circle is the writing-helping group that we talked about in the last chapter, where each writer shares and gets feedback and support for moving her or his words into public writing. And the small circles of the writing support groups ripple outward from there to the large Feather Circle of the whole class, where we listen in silent respect as we read our finished pieces.

I am convinced that what my Native American students have done and are doing can be done anywhere, in any writing classroom or group, by writers of any age. It does not take a $100,000 grant or a new textbook adoption or a resolution by the school board. It only takes a quiet belief in the power of people and words—and a reliance upon the heart's vision. And the rest will happen.

EXPLORATION

Saying Goodbye

When my third snail died, I said,
"I'm through with snails."
But I didn't mean it.

—FROM A POEM BY A THIRD-GRADER, AS REPORTED BY
KATHLEEN NORRIS IN *DAKOTA, A SPIRITUAL GEOGRAPHY*

Loss is a part of life. We lose many things: We lose our way in the dark; we lose our car keys; we lose our temper; we lose friends and loved ones. The Universe giveth and the Universe taketh away. Our losses need to be acknowledged, grieved, healed, cried for, laughed at.

Get quiet with your journal. Breathe deeply.

- **Take time to remember and acknowledge your losses.** Think of the people and the things that have gone from your life—through leaving or dying or moving on—through time and change.

- **List your losses in your journal as they come to your mind and heart.** Some will be obvious; some will wait quietly for your attention. List them like this:

    I remember losing . . .

      my grandmother, Annie
      my grandmother, Lydia
      my father—and finding him again
      Lorna, the first of my classmates to die
      my old black lab Fala from my boyhood hunting days
      the cottonwood tree by our driveway
      Joe, my best friend's alcoholic father . . .

- **Write freely about these losses in your journal.** What did they teach you, give you? How did they touch your life? What do you remember about them? What stories can you tell about them? Write. Write.

Toward Public Writing

Start by picking one of these losses that you have listed that you want to focus on for your public writing, and write further about it in your journal.

Then, eventually, write a public piece of some sort about this loss. Tell the story of your loss. Write a letter to that lost person or thing. Give your grieving a shape—turn your tears into art. Or do as Dreya did, for example, deftly weaving together a montage of losses in this piece:

Milk Carton

I have lost my place in a book. I have lied
and said I lost my report card. I have lost
my place in line and growled at the body
who slipped in when I wasn't looking. I have lost
my cool, kicked and thrown objects in fury,
I have lost my sense of time wandering in malls,
and come out blinking to find an afternoon
passed without notice. I have lost friends:
Bob to heroin, Bert to an embolism, Chrissy
to girls who didn't want me around. I have wondered
at lost children, their faces like blue oracles
on waxy milk cartons. I have lost touch,
standing awkwardly at receptions, the supermarket,
the gas station, wondering what to ask,

what to say. I lost the ruby pendant
that was my grandmother's; I still search for it
in my sleep. I have dreamt of losing my teeth,
falling, rolling out like marbles, leaving me
to lick my gums in sorrow. I have lost my nerve,
hanging up at the sound of his voice. I have sobbed,
grieving over lost boyfriends, but I can never lose
their names. I have lost my grip, reeling backwards.
I have lost hope, lost faith, and cried into the gap
these leave behind. I have lost memories, unable to recall
the dog, the babysitter, myself in my father's lap.
I have lost by brother who lost his heart,
drifting through jobs and cities like dreams;
I like to think he thinks sometimes of coming home,
of me.

Or focus on one loss, as Charles did when he wrote this memory-piece about a friend he lost in childhood:

I Remember

I remember when I was ten or eleven, and I lateraled a football to Leslie Johnson, and I watched him run gazelle-like past tacklers, looking as though he were skating on ice rather than running on grass.

I remember when Leslie and I played basketball together, and we were best friends, and our team was undefeated, and Leslie passed the ball to me, and I missed an easy lay-up, and we lost, and how nothing else mattered, and how he looked at me, and how he looked at me, and how he looked at me and turned away, and how I promised God and everyone that I'd never, ever, ever again miss practice.

I remember when I first heard Leslie was sick. It was at my brother's wedding, and I had talked with Mr. Dixon and asked about Leslie and he dropped his head and said, "Leslie isn't doing too well." And later I talked with my mom and she told me Leslie had MS and had come home to die and his mom had aged overnight and Mr. Dixon—Mr. Dixon!—had started to drink.

But most of all I remember sitting at the kitchen table, unable to write Leslie's parents, my hands trembling, grief and regret choking me, words wedged in my throat forcing me to gasp for breath, searching for words, wondering what to say to these neighbors, these friends, this mother and father whose prince had died.

As is always the case, the power in this piece comes from the honest words from Charles' heart as he gives this memory shape— and pays homage to his lost friend. You, too, can do what Dreya and Charles have done, as you work your losses into art.

EXPLORATION

Mythography

This Exploration honors the small stories you have been telling as you look back at the flow of your life, and puts them in a larger perspective. As you do this work, you will change to one degree or another because you will begin to see things about your past differently, to feel differently. Your heart will change. Your vision will change. In this Exploration, you will take an overview of the events and the turnings and learnings of your life, and a look at where you are now, and weave it all into a kind of myth-biography, a "mythography."

Slow down, breathe deeply, become still, center yourself.

- **In your mind, look back over the course of your life.** Reflect upon the turning points in your life's flow, upon the hurts and the scars and the joys. View the course of your life as though seeing it from above, and attend to the changes and the learnings that were happening within you.

- **In your journal, write a brief overview of the outer events of your life.** Draw a line down the center of your journal page. Write this overview on the left-hand side of the page. Write it in third person, as if you were looking at someone else's life. Begin with your birth, and briefly sketch the major events of your life—its high points and low points.

- **Write an internal synopsis of your life.** On the right-hand side of the page, write a parallel internal synopsis of what was going on inside you as these outer things were happening. Tell in a general way about what you were struggling with, what you were learning, how you were changing as your life moved along.

- **Reflect on where you are now in your life and what lies ahead.** Look upon the events of your life as lessons of some kind. Take time to reflect in your journal about what you have learned and how you have grown and changed from these lessons. Wonder about where and how you are now—and what your life to this point might have been preparing you to do and be.

Toward Public Writing

See what happens when you write a brief mythography (myth plus biography) of your life. Think of this as a kind of autobiography in a myth or fairy-tale mode. Do not worry over it; just play with it, have fun with it, see what it will teach you. Here are some directions, which, as always, you are free to ignore.

Using the general inner and outer movement of your life, write a myth-story of the life of this person (you) in third person. Give the person (yourself) a name other than your usual name, a symbolic name that feels appropriate or fitting. Then, as you look backward and inward, tell a story of the person's life.

You could work toward a finished mythography of 500 to 700 words. Give your story the feel of a myth or fairy tale or a child's story. Stay somewhat with the facts—let the story be based on the happenings of your own life—but be more concerned about the emotional truths of your life. Make your story lead to, end with, some sense of where you are now, how you are now, and how your unique past, no matter how hard or painful, has brought you to this moment.

Ruth, a dear friend and a former student, gave me the idea of writing a mythography in third person. To show you how a mythography might go, here is an excerpt from a piece she wrote in one of my classes:

Dream

In a time not so long ago, in a land not so far away, lived a pretty brown girl named Dream. Dream believed everything she was ever told—every Bible story her grandpa preached, everything about boys and girls her mama explained, every reason for being her favorite teacher taught. . . . Dream loved them all and she trusted their words.

One day she graduated from high school and became an "adult." That same week, she met a young man who had what her mother called "stability." He had a good job, a decent car, and money in the bank. He had the "good character" her grandpa preached about. And because he was a college graduate, he had "lots of potential," as her favorite teacher might say. So Dream's heart was filled with smiles. She got married, had children, and expected to live happily ever after.

Years passed and Dream's heart began to fill up with other stuff— disappointment, discouragement, bitterness, and fear. She was betrayed by her husband, and she no longer trusted the words of her loved ones. She searched all around her for other words she could trust—in self-help books, at church retreats, and in the mouths of friends. The words seemed true for the moment but failed when she tried to depend on them. The light of her smile grew dim. She had a sour taste in her mouth.

More years passed. By now she had worked two jobs, gone back to school, and raised her children with little help. She did not even notice the sour taste any more—she got used to it. Then one sunny day she walked down the street and was startled by the expression on the face of an old woman. The woman's twisted lips were drawn inward. Her face was mapped with wrinkles. . . . Dull gray eyes peered lifelessly. . . . The old woman walked haughtily, without love. This vision stopped Dream in her tracks. Quiet words whispered from the stillness of her mind: "See what bitterness will do." She felt the sour taste in her mouth and saw her future.

That very same hour Dream went home and looked in the mirror. Her face was sad, but there were as yet no bitter lines. She was thankful. A smile filled her face. She decided to let disappointment go and the sour taste with it. She somehow knew it was all right to look for words to believe in. She remembered that her own quiet words surfaced when her mind was still. So, instead of anxiously searching for words all around her, she began to calmly search within. . . .

"She began to calmly search within." Yes. A good place to be. Ruth's writing helped her get to that point, and her story helps those with whom she shares it. Write your own mythography and see what happens for you.

EXPLORATION

Writing and Praying

As you do this writing-and-being work, you will begin to know that you are more than you have been taught you are. You will begin to get in touch with your inner Self, your inner needs. You will begin to move and change and grow naturally, like a seedling seeking the sunlight.

This does not mean that your life will suddenly become easy. You will still struggle, hurt, cry, get angry, know fear. I like to remember that "Jesus wept." One of my favorite stories about him is the one where he angrily drives the money-suckers out of the temple. And while Buddha was sitting under the bodhi tree seeking enlightenment, they say, ants built nests in his hair.

There is a Buddhist saying about such change: "Before enlightenment, chopping wood, pumping water. After enlightenment, chopping wood, pumping water." The work goes on. The change is inside.

As you do this writing-and-being work, you will see your struggles differently. Instead of denying them, you will be working your way through them toward the sunlight of love.

The following Exploration will lead you into writing a prayer, into praying in your journal and in your life. As you get into this journal process, your writing may sometimes start to sound like prayers, in the best sense of that word: prayers that acknowledge your struggles and seek clearer vision, that open yourself to better being, that give thanks for great gifts and small joys.

This Exploration invariably causes strong reactions. People who pride themselves on their atheism or agnosticism and people who have run from the small religion that was forced upon them in childhood bristle and say, in effect, "I will be damned if I will write a prayer." And people who have a small self comfortably ensconced within some rigidly defined dogma smile in easy delight and begin rattle-writing off rote and empty words. Neither discovers anything.

I caution you to watch yourself as you do this Exploration. Watch what bothers you about it. Watch out for easy, patterned words. Pray your own words, not the words of others. Make a new definition of prayer, your own definition. Wonder what a prayer might be—and to whom, and why. Stay open to the possibilities of prayer. Wonder. Watch. Explore.

To prepare, be still for an extended time: Sit in silent breathing for five or ten minutes.

- **Turn quietly to your journal and write a prayer.** Write a prayer to God, to Yahweh, to the Great Spirit, to Mother Earth, to the Universe. Write to let go of the things you need to release, things that are hurting and overwhelming you. Write to open yourself to the things you need. Write to give thanks for great gifts and small joys.

  Make praying a regular practice in your journal work and see what happens. See how you feel and what you resent and whom you address and what feels awkward or comfortable. And stay open, stay open, stay open. . . .

Toward Public Writing

From your private prayers, from your prayer work in your journal, write a prayer to share with others, to read or pray aloud with your class, group, family, or friends. Write a prayer from your heart, from your hurt, from your need. Write a prayer and see what happens. Write a prayer and dare to share it with others, dare to pray it.

There are 10,000 ways to pray. Here is Alison's prayer:

A Difficult Assignment

How can I pray? I prayed a lot until I was twenty-five. I thought that was enough.

My prayers since that time have been more like:
    Please, God, don't let her be in a car wreck.
    Do not let him kill himself.
    Please do not let Rascal die.
        I cannot get along without him.
    Let this be a bad dream.
    Help Mama get well
        and I will be a better person.
    Let Daddy live forever.

I cannot pray to the God of my childhood. He is not around any more.

I cannot pray to the all-purpose Unitarian god. She does not believe in our doing this.

I cannot pray to the Great Spirit. I do not know who that is.

I do not know Buddha, Jesus, Mohammed, Vishnu, Shiva,

Brahma, or any assorted goddesses. Maybe I will know some
of them next week or next year—but not now.

Since I always do my assignments, I will use my grandmother's
dinner blessing (with a slight alteration and a short addition):

A Prayer
Father/Mother, make us thankful for these and all our
blessings and take care of our loved ones wherever they are.
And bless the sun, the moon, the stars, the Earth, and
everyone on it, and help us to save our sisters and brothers and
our planet.

Amen.

Thank you, Alison (and your grandmother), for the honesty of
your words and for your prayer, which prays for us all.

Here is Debbi's prayer:

today's prayer
I give you my prayer, my day,
*   my attitude, my heart,*
*   my pain, my stomachache,*
*   my love, my night*
I give you my fear, my desire,
*   my inability to think clearly,*
*   my wisdom, my ignorance,*
*   my energy, my lethargy,*
*   my ambition, my blue flannel sheets*
I surrender to the arms of the sky
*   to the well that leads us to each other*
*   and the stream that connects us*

I breathe in the sunrise, the green grass,
    the crescent moon and venus,
    the geraniums and chrysanthemums,
    the smell of wet dogs and manure
I pray for peace
    for the families being murdered . . .
        in Central America, Beijing, South Africa
    for my student
        whose sister was shot to death
        by her husband in a parking lot
    for children
        whose parents drink
    for the children in the newspaper
        killed by their own parents
I pray for peace
    for my grandfather
        who stopped opening birthday
        and Christmas gifts after his wife died
    for my mother
        who was told to walk five feet behind
        her husband on their honeymoon . . .
    for my brother
        struggling with yuppiehollowness
I pray for peace in my home, peace
    for Joan
    for my dogs and cats
        who want to be in when they're
        out and out when they're in,
        and have Purina when
        they have something else

and something else when
they have Purina
for my screaming selves

fill me with
   peace
      appreciation
         kindness
            patience
               love

                  thank you

I like Debbi's prayer. I like its reverence and irreverence. Debbi's and Alison's prayers help me to pray. Let them help you.

ten

CLOSING

There has been no miracle cure except the everyday miracle of opening my eyes and seeing the world before me—and working very hard.

A Prayer and a Plan

I leave you now. By way of saying goodbye, I want to tell you a story. It is a story that feels appropriate for what I want to say to you now. It is about writing and being. It has found its way out of my journal and into these words for you and for me:

Just a little while ago, I came home from another long day of dancing and fighting with the world. I opened the windows of the house. Then I cut up some vegetables and put them in the oven to bake. Now I am sitting at my desk in the bedroom, writing, trying to turn the jumbled numbness in my mind into something meaningful to say to you. . . .

I watched the evening news for awhile, but I soon turned it off. I do not feel strong enough tonight to watch more footage of bodies bloody from terrorist bombs. I do not want to hear about drive-by shootings and drug raids. Tonight, I am too tired to try to reconcile the image of a starving child in Ethiopia with the Love Boat Cruise commercial that follows.

In the face of that, in the face of all the seemingly mindless madness in the world, what can I say to you? What can we say to each other?

So I sit here at my journal. Through the open bedroom window, I can hear the muffled roar of the traffic on the freeway. But I can also hear the resident mockingbird on the power line above the alley, going through his lengthy repertoire, singing as if he were in heaven, singing in spite of the madness of this world.

And right outside the window in the garden, the tiny seed that I planted three months ago is now an eight-foot-tall sunflower. The yellow and brown blossom at the top, larger than my hand, is facing west this evening, into the setting sun. Tomorrow, when I get up to run before dawn, it will be facing the east, waiting.

And today, down at the reservation, I thought I had to hurry to get back to a meeting at the university. Then Vicki asked if we could talk, and I knew I needed only to be there.

We went outside and sat under the eucalyptus tree at the weathered picnic table covered with graffiti. Vicki spoke softly, almost in a whisper, but the words poured out of her. She talked about not knowing her real parents, about being adopted, about being molested by her adoptive father from the time she was seven. She talked about being put into a foster home, where she was again abused. And she talked about her confusion now, about being fif-teen years old and seven months pregnant by a guy who has run off somewhere.

But in all of her words, I could hear no hatred, no self-pity—I could just see two tears that slid slowly down her face when she talked about her unborn baby. Later, as we walked back to the classroom, she slipped her hand into mine, like a friend and like the child that she still is. . . .

That is how it went today. And now I need to say something to you about where I am and what it's all about. When I started writing, I felt I had nothing to say in the face of violence and ter-rorism and child abuse and the other daily atrocities of our lives. I was just pouring out my hurt and anger and frustration. But in the middle of this madness, I also found a miraculous sunflower and a defiant mockingbird and a courageous fifteen-year-old who is about to bring a baby into this world.

And if you stop to think about it, right in the middle of all this madness, right here in the people and things of our daily lives, you and I have the power to create a little world that not only is not mad but has within it a bit of peace and love and meaning.

What better thing to do in the world at this time? What a great gift—for ourselves and for the world. So here is a prayer and a plan:

Let us not, you and I, be paralyzed by the sometimes madness of the world. Let us follow our writing and our being inward to that quiet place within ourselves and let us be centered there.

And from that center,

let us go outward in love to the world.

Let us plant sunflowers

and listen for mockingbirds
and prepare a place for Vicki's baby. . . .

All my relations . . .
—GLN

EXPLORATION

Where Are You Now? (Part 2 of 2)

Find an hour or so to be alone with your journal. Open the envelope containing the writing you did for the "Where Are You Now? (Part 1)" Exploration at the end of Chapter 1. Read carefully what you wrote there, reflecting on the person you were then, sensing the person you are now, and wondering about your change and growth and becoming.

Close your eyes and just be still for awhile. Then, consider the following questions. (These are the same kinds of questions you answered in Part 1 of this Exploration, but do not be limited by them.) In your journal, write freely and openly and wonderingly again about these things:

- **How are you feeling about yourself (your Self and selves) now?** What has changed?

- **How does your past feel to you now?** Have your feelings changed? How does your past feel different to you now?

- **What do you value in your life now?** What feels good, positive, strong in your life now? Who matters to you now? Who are the important people in your life now? How has this changed?

- **What are your dreams, goals, needs now?** How have they changed?

- **What is happening to you spiritually?** Are you sensing your Center, your Self, beyond the little struggling selves? How has this changed for you?

You can do this kind of writing at the end of each journal, as you complete it. Or you can do it at the end of your time in a class or writing group, as a kind of closure. It can also be transposed onto loose paper and sealed in an envelope to start the process all over again—a kind of ongoing attending to the changing, growing state of yourself.

Toward Public Writing

If you are doing this Exploration with others at the end of the meetings of a journal group or a writing class, you can work your personal writing into a piece of public writing and share with the others your observations and reflections.

Here, for example, are some excerpts from a courageous and honest sharing that Helen wrote at the end of our semester together:

Dearest Class,
. . . It feels good to look at myself today and see me feeling stable and peaceful. But reading the envelope writing we did in January brought me face to face with someone I had worked very hard to forget.
When I began this class, my mild drug use had become a daily problem. . . . It is a hard self for me to look back on. There was no sordid descent into shooting galleries and

addiction, just one moment of awakening to realize that I was standing alone in the women's room at work, trying to balance the coke and the tooter while I shoveled in the white dust. I remember lying to my dad, telling him someone had broken into the car, when actually I had locked my keys in, gotten drunk, and put my fist through the window to get them out. . . .

To begin the class, I took out our assignment, did two lines of coke, got miserably depressed, and wrote about a sentence on each of the suggested topics. This new beginning was a humble one. It was so hard to call up the words to describe the situation I was in—the holes and stains on the walls, the tattered rug, the ancient space heater that was my only furniture, screaming fights upstairs, the drunken ghost of my father haunting the night deadalive. . . .

About Dad I wrote, "Dad's drinking lately. A whale of a drunk the other night, starting on a bottle I'd bought." That's all I wrote. But those short sentences were cracks that burst the floodgates. I was so very much helped in stopping my denial, for the first time in my life, by Lynn's sharing and by Karyn's sharing and by everybody's sharing and by everybody's acceptance of sharing.

. . . What I remember best (and feared the most) was at the end. The last sentence read: "Spiritual beliefs." That is at the top of the second page of my envelope writing, and beneath it is what looks like an endless expanse of white, blank space. It wasn't that I had no spiritual beliefs, just that I had lost faith in their ability to sustain me and in my ability to sustain myself. "Sad sad bottomless sad," I called myself. I had no grounding.

*There has been no miracle cure, except the everyday
miracle of opening my eyes and seeing the world before me,
and working very hard. . . . I wish I could tell you all how
much you helped. I used to pull out your thank-you notes to
me every day. Sometimes more but never less than once a day,
I would read them, just to hear someone else saying I was okay.*

*. . . I keep many masks clamped on firmly, suffocatingly.
But here and now I have taken a few off. Sometimes the faces
underneath are very ugly, but I saw no one in class recoil in
disgust. So maybe I'll continue to loosen the screws. I don't
know. I don't expect miracles, except the everyday ones. . . .*

*There are other ways I'd prefer to be remembered by the
people here. But I promised myself, months ago, to be as
honest as I could with each assignment. I'd like to say I wrote
and read this to help others in their struggles. Sure, that's
there. But I did this for me.*

ALL MY LOVE, HELEN

This is the way we grow. This is the writing-and-being process.
I wish you well in your journal journey toward peace and love.

Teacher's Guide to the Explorations

The Explorations in this book have many uses in teaching public writing. Here are some of those uses:

EXPLORATION	USES	PAGE
Exploring Your Epigraph	Being specific Letting content find form Avoiding generalizations and abstractions	41
Collecting Small Joys	Tightening-no wasted words Showing rather than telling Sense of form	50
Freeing the Writer Within	Narrative as discovery Finding form Being specific	62
Word Photos	Tightening Focus Imagery	65
Who Am I?	Point of view Dialogue Quotations	80
Talking to Your Selves	Beginning and closure Dialogue Point of view Using dramatic form	83
Maps and Memories	Find stories within Finding form to fit content	95

References

Blake, William. *Poetry and Prose of William Blake*. Garden City: Doubleday, 1965.

Castaneda, Carlos. *Journey to Ixtlan: The Lessons of Don Juan*. New York: Pocket Books, 1972.

cummings, e.e. *Collected Poems*. New York: Harcourt, Brace, 1938.

Frank, Anne. *Anne Frank: The Diary of a Young Girl*. New York: Pocket Books, 1952.

Hooper, Judith, and Dick Teresi. *The Three-Pound Universe*. New York: Macmillan, 1986.

Lee, Harper. *To Kill a Mockingbird*. New York: Popular Library, 1962.

McGinn, Bernard, ed. *Meister Eckhart: Teacher and Preacher*. New York: Paulist Press, 1986.

Merton, Thomas. *Raids on the Unspeakable*. New York: New Directions, 1964.

Momaday, N. Scott. *House Made of Dawn*. New York: New American Library, 1966.

Neihardt, John. *Black Elk Speaks*. Lincoln: University of Nebraska Press, 1961. (This is the best source for the words and wisdom of Black Elk.)

Pirsig, Robert. *Zen and the Art of Motorcycle Maintenance*. New York: Morrow, 1974.

Sagan, Carl. *The Dragons of Eden*. New York: Random House, 1977.

Suzuki, Shunryu. *Zen Mind, Beginner's Mind*. New York: John Weatherhill, Inc., 1979.

Selected Bibliography

Into the sometimes small world of academic writing, these are some of the books that have reached in wholeness to further my writing and being:

Aroniw, Nancy Slonim. *Writing from the Heart: Tapping the Power of Your Inner Voice*. New York: Hyperion, 1998.

Baldwin, Christina. *Life's Companion: Journal Writing as Spiritual Quest*. New York: Bantam Books, 1991.

Baldwin, Christina. *One to One: Self-Understanding through Journal Writing*. New York: M. Evans, 1977.

Borkin, Susan. *Writing From Inside Out*. Los Altos, CA: Center for Personal Growth and Development, 1995.

Bradbury, Ray. *Zen in the Art of Writing*. Santa Barbara, CA: Capra Press, 1990.

Cameron, Julie. *The Artist's Way: A Spiritual Path to Higher Creativity*. New York: Tarcher Putnam, 1992.

Capacchione, Lucia. *The Creative Journal: The Art of Finding Yourself*. Hollywood: Newcastle Publishing, 1992.

Capacchione, Lucia. *The Well-Being Journal: Drawing on Your Inner Power to Heal Yourself*. Hollywood: Newcastle Publishing, 1989.

Cerwinski, Laura. *Writing as a Healing Art: The Transforming Power of Self-Expression*. New York: Perigree, 1999.

Field, Joanna. *A Life of One's Own*. Los Angeles: Jeremy P. Tarcher, 1981.

Fletcher, Ralph. *Breathing In, Breathing Out: Keeping a Writer's Notebook*. Portsmouth, NH: Heinemann, 1996.

Goldberg, Natalie. *Wild Mind: Living the Writer's Life*. New York: Bantam Books, 1990.

Goldberg, Natalie. *Writing Down the Bones: Freeing the Writer Within*. Boston & London: Shambhala, 1986.

Heard, Georgia. *Writing Toward Home*. Portsmouth, NH: Heinemann, 1996.

Keyes, Ralph. *The Courage to Write*. New York: Henry Holt & Co., 1995.

Klauser, Henriette Anne. *Writing on Both Sides of the Brain*. San Francisco: Harper & Row, 1987.

Lamott, Anne. *bird by bird: Some Instructions on Writing and Life*. New York: Doubleday, 1994.

L'Engle, Madeleine. *Walking on Water: Reflections on Faith and Art*. LaBelle, FL: Harold Shaw Publishers, 1980.

Lu Chi. Sam Hamill, trans. *Art of Writing: Lu Chi's Wen Fu*. Minneapolis: Milkweed Editions, 1991.

Macrorie, Kenneth. *Telling Writing*. Portsmouth, NH: Boyton Cook Publishers, 1985.

Maisel, Eric. *Deep Writing: 7 Principles that Bring Ideas to Life*. New York: Tarcher, 1999.

Metzger, Deena. *Writing for Your Life*. San Francisco: Harper SF, 1992.

Momaday, N. Scott. *The Man Made of Words*. New York: St. Martins, 1997.

Progoff, Ira. *At a Journal Workshop: The Basic Text and Guide for Using the Intensive Journal Process*. New York: Dialogue House, 1975.

Rico, Gabrielle. *Writing the Natural Way: Using Right-Brain Techniques to Release Your Expressive Powers*. Los Angeles: Jeremy P. Tarcher, 1983.

Rainer, Tristine. *The New Diary: How to Use a Journal for Self-Guidance and Expanded Creativity*. Los Angeles: Jeremy P. Tarcher, 1979.

See, Caroline. *Making A Literary Life: Advice for Writers and Other Dreamers*. New York: Random House, 2002.

Simons, George. *Keeping Your Personal Journal*. New York: Ballantine Books, 1986.

Sjher, Gail. *The Intuitive Writer: Listening to Your Own Voice*. New York: Penguin, 2002.

Solly, Richard, and Roseann Lloyd. *Journey Notes: Writing for Recovery and Spiritual Growth*. San Francisco: Harper & Row, 1989.

Ueland, Brenda. *If You Want to Write*. St. Paul, MN: Schubert Club, 1983.

Waldman, Mark, ed. *The Spirit of Writing: Classic and Contemporary Essays Celebrating the Writing Life*. New York: Tarcher, 2001.

Wooldridge, Susan Goldsmith. *Poemcrazy*. New York: Three Rivers Press, 1996.

Made in the USA
Lexington, KY
03 September 2014